THE LOST JESUS SCROLL

The Lost Jesus Scroll

*Buried for Centuries
in the Archives of the Vatican*

Elizabeth MacDonald Burrows

SEABOARD PRESS
AN IMPRINT OF J. A. ROCK & CO., PUBLISHERS

The Lost Jesus Scroll by Elizabeth MacDonald Burrows

SEABOARD PRESS

is an imprint of James A. Rock & Company, Publishers

The Lost Jesus Scroll copyright ©2006, 2007 by
Elizabeth MacDonald Burrows

Special contents of this edition copyright ©2007
by Seaboard Press

All applicable copyrights and other rights reserved worldwide. No part of this publication may be reproduced, in any form or by any means, for any purpose, except as provided by the U.S. Copyright Law, without the express, written permission of the publisher.

Address comments and inquiries to:
SEABOARD PRESS
9710 Traville Gateway Drive, #305
Rockville, MD 20850

E-mail:
jrock@rockpublishing.com   lrock@rockpublishing.com
Internet URL: www.rockpublishing.com

Trade Paperback
ISBN: 1-59663-528-2
978-1-59663-528-9

Library of Congress Control Number: 2006931632

Printed in the United States of America

First Edition: 2007

Dedicated to

The Master who

walked the hills of Galilee

*My gratitude to those
who helped to make this book possible:*

Professor Edmond S. Bordeaux,

and

*Santosh Boddikuri
Michelle Dossett
Peter Hiatt
Gordon James
Gordon and Claudia Majack
Cheryl McLaine
Ray & Chio Nakanishi
Mary Ransdell
Ralph & Betty Sand III
Ralph & Yvonne Sand II
Michael Shemett
Cheryl Watkins
Keith Wong*

TABLE OF CONNTS

Introduction xiii

Chapter I
    The Great Discovery 1

Chapter II
    The Essene Secrecy 11

Chapter III
    Keys to Understanding the Lost Jesus Scroll 21

Chapter IV
    The Essene Code of the Angels 29

SECTION ONE
    Mysteries of the Forces of Earth 35

    Chapter One
        Son of Heaven – Son of Earth 37

    Chapter Two
        The Mysteries of Nature 41

    Chapter Three
        Man Cannot Serve Two Masters 47

    Chapter Four
        Three Paths of Purification 51

    Chapter Five
        The One Law 55

    Chapter Six
        Natural Healing 59

    Chapter Seven
        Law of Life 65

    Chapter Eight
        Foods in Their Season 71

    Chapter Nine
        Jesus' Seven Pathways to Inner Peace 75

SECTION TWO

Fellowship with the Angels 85
Introduction 87
Jesus on Fellowship 89

First Invocation
    Power (Creation of the Universe) 93

Second Invocation
    The Sun (Giver of Life) 96

Third Invocation
    Love (Cohesive Force of the Universe) 98

Fourth Invocation
    Water (Sustainer of Life) 102

Fifth Invocation
    Wisdom (Directive Power of the Universe) 104

Sixth Invocation
    Air (Life Force) 108

Seventh Invocation
    Eternal Life (Immortality of the Soul) 110

Eighth Invocation
    Earth (The Holy Mother) 113

Ninth Invocation
    Creative Work (Highway to Heaven) 116

Tenth Invocation
    Live (God's Visible Expression) 121

Eleventh Invocation
    Peace (Living in Harmony) 124

Twelfth Invocation
    Joy (Gateway to Happiness) 127

Thirteenth Invocation
    God (Oneness with all Life) 130

Fourteenth Invocation
    The Holy Earth (Union of Heaven and Earth) 136

SECTION THREE
  Jesus' Teachings on Merger with Three Sacred Rivers
    (Life – Sound – Light) 139
  Merger with The Sacred Rivers 141

Bibliography 149
Index 153

INTRODUCTION

Thirty years have passed since beginning my search for the real Jesus. During this time I have not ceased in my endeavor to trace the fragments of the Master's life through 2,000 years of historical and biblical documents. No investigator has ever approached his life more diligently, or more thoroughly, for my search has been governed by my heart and uncluttered by pre-conceived concepts. I became consumed by questions, as to what he ate, how he dressed, where he was between the ages of one and three, three and twelve and twelve and thirty-three. Nonetheless, nothing that I discovered took away from the magnificence or purpose of his death. Rather I developed a greater passion for more knowledge as a result of my efforts.

When I first started my research I little knew that I had begun an investigation that would eventually span three decades. Now I wonder what I might have thought had I known that I, who had found history an intolerable subject in school, would ultimately peruse manuscripts from all parts of the world, including rare translated manuscripts from the Secret Archives of the Roman Vatican.

During the early years of my search for the real Jesus, the largest and most important piece of the great puzzle fell into place. It became apparent that the Master taught two teachings; one to the masses and another to his close followers. These hidden teachings instantly captured my heart, and ultimately changed the course of my life. They are so powerful and universal that they are alone sufficient to abolish all religious and racial differences.

The early period of my exploration into the life of Jesus of Nazareth was probably more revelation than documentation, somewhat like a dawn breaking through the last threads of night. As one of my great teachers, Professor Edmond S. Bordeaux, said, the common or popular literal interpretation of the scripture "did not always correlate with the reality."

Jesus sometimes appeared to be a Jesus partially created from human comprehension, subject to exoteric understanding. I had set out to find the truth behind ritual, however, and left no stone unturned regarding either Jesus or his teachings. There had to be answers somewhere and, of course, there were. Eventually I found that many explanations were tied into the seeming duality of heaven and earth. While each living thing, including man appears distinct and separate; this seems to be somewhat of an illusion. I would discover that matter is none other than the dense outer cloak of spirit; or in simple language, the suit of clothes which God wears.

It did not take too long to determine that Jesus teachings could be understood on multiple levels and that his more popular teachings were literal and related to basic human comprehension. Accordingly, theories that were not in harmony with the essential nature of the universe were discarded.. Having acquired this knowledge I returned to my studies. Everything the Master taught took on a different meaning, and what had once been a knotted ball of string became straight as a new course to follow was laid out in front of me. To summarize my findings would take many years of writing and teaching. For this reason I have chosen to dedicate myself to the *Lost Jesus Scroll,* as I believe it will most benefit the world at this time.

Evidence of Christianity's secret teachings is replete in the writings of the early church fathers, such as St. Dionysius, the first Bishop of Athens, who said, "The tradition of the sacrament is said to have been divided into three Degrees, or grades; purification, initiation, and accomplishment of perfection."

The Apostolic Constitution attributed to Clemens, Bishop of Rome, described the early church (AD 347), saying. "These regulations must on no account be communicated to all sorts of persons, because of the Mysteries contained in them."

Tertullian (AD 216} stated in his Apology, "None are admitted to the religious Mysteries without an oath of secrecy. We are especially bound to this caution, because if we prove faithless, we should not only provoke Heaven, but also draw upon our heads the utmost rigor of human displeasure. Far hence, ye profane, is the prohibition from all holy Mysteries."

Archelaus, Bishop of Cascara in Mesopotamia, who in the year 278, initiated a controversy with the Manichaeans said: "These Mysteries are not explained to the Gentiles at all, nor are they taught openly in the hearing of Catechumens: but much that is spoken is in disguised terms, that the Faithful who posses the knowledge may be still more informed and those not acquainted with it, may suffer no disadvantage."

The list goes on to include such Bishops as Cyril, Bishop of Jerusalem, St. Basil, the Great Bishop of Caesarea, St. Ambrose, Archbishop of Milan, and St Augustine, Bishop of Hippo.

Nevertheless, the words of St. Cyril, appointed Bishop of Alexandria in 412 AD, best sum up the reason for the secrecy. In his 7th Book against Julian, he writes: "These Mysteries are so profound and so exalted, that they can be comprehended only by those who are enlightened. I shall not, therefore, attempt to speak of what is so admirable in them, lest by revealing them to the uninitiated I should offend against the injunction not to give what is holy to the impure, nor cast pearls before such as cannot estimate their worth.

"I should say much more if I were not afraid of being heard by those who are uninitiated: because men are apt to deride what they do not understand. And the ignorant, not being aware of the weakness of their minds, condemn what they ought most to venerate."

When I chanced to stumble upon the *Lost Jesus Scroll*, I found myself in the same quandary as those who had established the early church. If I attempted to reveal it, would I also open myself to inevitable criticism? Yet, if I did not reveal the lost teachings would the wrong already imposed upon the Christian religion be perpetuated?

The greatest and most closely guarded of the secret teachings, those associated not only with Jesus, but with Moses as well, appear to be those surrounding the impenetrable mysteries pertaining to the transformation of human to divine. Although St. John clearly outlines this process in Revelation, Jesus teaches, not only that every human being can achieve it, but also how they can achieve it. This represents the very core of the *Lost Scroll*. Certainly no other work in the history of religion or philosophy better explains how the divine nature of mankind can be raised and human life transformed.

It is my personal belief that the discovery of the *Lost Jesus Scroll*, long buried in the Hidden Archives of the Roman Vatican is one of the greatest religious finds of the Twentieth Century.

—*Elizabeth MacDonald Burrows*

CHAPTER I

The Great Discovery
Discovery of "The Lost Jesus Scroll"

In 1970, after being deeply touched by the dissention between people and wars between nations, I began a search into the nature of the universe. It was not long before I became fascinated with the life of Jesus, for he was a man of peace and a man for all nations, but above all he was a man of God. I felt that somewhere in his teachings I would find a mysterious key or some answer that would guide me through the maze of religious controversy. During the three decades of research on Jesus' life which followed I made many discoveries, most not commonly known to the masses of today's world. Among these were the translations of his death warrant, a transcript of his court trial and an intense exploration into some of his secret teachings.

After a few years of research I could usually spot possible forgeries quite easily. Jesus had a certain way of speaking, as well as an deep understanding of natural and cosmic law. This made it impossible for an unenlightened person to understand, let alone duplicate. Because Jesus' teachings are multitudinous and can be understood at multiple levels they often appear to have a dual meaning, whether one is perusing tradition or some ancient manuscript. One aspect of his teaching appears simple and designed for mass consciousness. The other is a deeper and more complex revelation, and usually best understood by those people who have sought for answers to life through an enlightened mind.

The secret transformation of human to divine has become one the most protected secrets of Christendom, in the past by intent, and in recent centuries, perhaps through ignorance. I am quite certain it would have also remained hidden to me, had I not inadvertently been brought face-to-face with such a possibility during my in-depth study of St. John's Revelation. It was readily obvious during my efforts to break the code of Revelation that many of St. John's beasts and dragons never really existed, nor would they exist in the future. "Why then did he go into such elaborate symbolism," I wondered, unless there was another, but buried meaning amid the bottomless pit and fiery brimstone.

At the time I had not come across the *Lost Jesus Scroll*, nor unraveled many of the great mysteries of Christendom. However, I certainly knew that the latter existed, and believed that I had discovered the master key for unlocking them.

While researching, what I like to refer to as the "Jesus mysteries," another shadow crossed my path that further complicated my investigation. During this long and intensive perusal of Jesus' life, I found myself facing a very perplexing problem. Apparently there had been a number of different men named Jesus throughout Jewish history. Some had preceded the Master, others lived approximately at the same time, and one, or two, came later.

The complete works of Flavius Josephus, a respected Jewish Historian, is replete with references concerning the numerous people who bore that name. In his writings Josephus mentions the following: Jesus, the son of Phabet deprived of the high-priesthood, Jesus, son of Ananus, Jesus, the son of Sapphias, governor of Tiberias, Jesus brother of Onias, deprived of the high priesthood by Antiochus Epiphanes, Jesus, son of Gamaliel, made high priest, Jesus, the eldest priest after Ananus, Jesus, son of Damneus made high priest, Jesus, son of Gamala, Jesus, the son of Saphat, ringleaders of the robbers and Jesus, son of Thebuthus, a priest.

To further complicate this already growing state of confusion, the *Lost Jesus Scroll* produced yet one more apparent Jesus. He was, and still is, referred to by many as the Essene Jesus. Today, this Jesus has a rather large following that call themselves the *New Essenes*. Although the sect claims to follow the teachings in the *Jesus Scroll*, they also believe that that their *Jesus* was never crucified and that he was a life-long member of the ancient Essene Sect.

The primary controversy surrounding Jesus' life for me seemed to exist between the man they called Jesus the Christ and the man who became known as the Essene Jesus. Both had lived at the same time. My confusion over these two had been further intensified by the fact that my research produced some pretty strong evidence that these were not two different men, but rather one man. One day, after floundering for weeks amid the dusty labyrinths of research, I found myself with an intense case of what I call, *mental indigestion..* Although there was no one to hear me, I literally screamed out "Will the real Jesus please stand up."

Unfortunately the Biblical scriptures gave no evidence whatsoever that Jesus the Christ had ever been associated with the Essene Sect. Biblical history, however, also contains many gaping holes in the continuity of the Master's life; far too many to rule out the possibility that there might be a link. As I grappled with the chronological placement of the numerous Jesus' I decided it would be necessary to fill in many of the missing pieces of this giant puzzle before I could learn the real truth. Who was Jesus the Christ?

Methodically, I began to rule out the various members of the Jewish sect named Jesus one-by-one, placing each in their proper historical time period. Eventually I was left with only two, but they were the same two that had plagued me for days: Jesus the Christ and the Essene Jesus. I began to wonder if I had made any real headway in resolving the issue.

It was not the dual teachings of Jesus the Christ that provided my most intense frustration, but the Essene Jesus, who also taught both an exoteric and esoteric teaching. It was virtually impossible to distinguish the difference between the two. By this time I had traveled many roads in search of truth, for it is my belief that no research should be based only on what is traditional and acceptable. Therefore, never ruling out any potential clue, regardless of its improbability, I continued. There appeared but one way to ferret the greater story, and that was with an open mind and without preconceived ideas.

Although it took hundreds of hours to sift through all of the material collected over the years, such as, *The Letter*, written by an eyewitness to the crucifixion seven years after Jesus was crucified, *Confession of Pontius Pilate* and the *Apocryphal New Testament*, I felt it necessary to do so. Had I pursued my research with a closed mind and preconceived standards I would not have chanced upon one of the greatest discoveries of the Twentieth Century—the *Lost Jesus Scroll*. Its entry into my life made it possible for me to prove that the Essene Jesus and Jesus the Christ was one and the same person.

Contact with the *Lost Jesus Scroll* occurred during the early part of my first United States lecture tour. During my appearance in the beautiful city of San Diego, I was presented with a translation and modification of an ancient Vatican manuscript containing some unknown teachings of Jesus. Professor Edmond S. Bordeaux, who had done the original translation of the scroll, had been a Professor at the University of Cluj. He was also a well-known Philologist, as well as an expert in fifteen languages, including Hebrew and Aramaic. Although one's first inclination might be to relegate such material to the Gnostic writings, or to one of the many attempts to rationalize the so-called *lost years* of Jesus' life, this particular work immediately touched me in a special way.

There were two major reasons for my interest: one, the translation correlated with other rare manuscripts I had come in contact with during my years of research, and two, I was unable to find one single flaw in the actual application of its content. Jesus' teachings on the transformation of human to divine seemed to systematically reveal a path to oneness with God.

The only sure way to fully evaluate this new material was to ascertain whether the work was authentic. Therefore, I applied directly to the Roman Vatican for permission to have some scholar do an independent translation, for I could not speak Aramaic, Hebrew, or Greek, much less translate it. At the same time, it also seemed important to contact Professor Bordeaux, who had done the original translation, editing, and modification of the Hebrew and Aramaic Texts.

Immediately, I put the teachings in the *Jesus Scroll* into active practice. The more I worked with them the more certain I became that the scroll was not a forgery. It had the usual simplicity of an outer teaching, yet the complexity of an inner teaching, so distinctive in Jesus' other works. It also revealed certain aspects of natural and cosmic law that went far beyond the knowledge of the average human. Either the manuscript was what it claimed to be or had been written by some highly enlightened individual.

During this time I was successful in my attempt to find Professor Bordeaux and to inquire into the circumstances that ultimately led him to the discovery of this rare work. I was extremely pleased, when a short time later I received several typewritten pages summarizing his discovery. I was further impressed by Professor's background. He had earned a Ph.D. from Sorbonne in Biochemistry, and subsequent degrees in the fields of Psychology, Archaeology, and Philosophy from the Universities of Vienna and Leipzig. He was obviously very reputable, and certainly capable of translating such a rare manuscript.

According to the material I received from the Professor, he had apparently translated, edited, and modified the *Lost Jesus Scroll* during his early studies in the Roman Vatican. He explained in his letter to me, that the entire manuscript existed both in Aramaic and Hebrew in the Secret Archives of the Roman Vatican, and also in old Slavonic in the Royal Archives of the Habsburgs (now the property of the Austrian Government).

Professor's letter, which pertained to the discovery of the *Lost Scroll,* began at the time he graduated magna cum laude and valedictorian at the age of eighteen from a Catholic monastery of the Pairist Order. Following his graduation, the young Edmond had been called into the office of the headmaster, Monsignor Mondik, who was then Prior of the monastery. Apparently Monsignor recognized the astuteness of young Edmond and felt that the youth might follow the wayward paths of other young men of his time if he did not intercede. Thus, he offered Edmond a letter of introduction, which would allow him to meet Monsignor Mercati, then Prefect of the Archives of the Roman Vatican. This was not without a price, however, for Edmond would have to subject himself to the vows of poverty, chastity, and obedience of the Franciscan Monks.

Having accepted these conditions, the young scholar soon found himself studying in the labyrinths of the Roman Vatican. At first he was intensely engrossed in the life of his favorite saint, St. Francis of Assisi. Soon, however, the youth was cautioned by the Prefect to desist in his intense research on the Saint, saying that St. Francis was merely the ocean. He, Edmond, must now search for the river, the stream, and the source, which ultimately led him to the works of St. Benedict (the river) and of St. Jerome (the stream).

During his research on the life of St. Benedict young Edmond found references to the Saint's translation of some mysterious Hebrew fragments. These writings had apparently been derived from the peaceful teachings of an ancient Brotherhood called the Essenes and had been destroyed by the ravages of war, although enough important fragments survived to enable the youth to correlate St. Benedict's *Regula Santa* with the teachings of St. Jerome.

Turning his attention to St. Jerome, Professor Bordeaux soon discovered that Jerome had also found some ancient manuscripts fragments, which had been in the possession of a few Jewish hermits and Rabbis. Once again, these writings referred to a Brotherhood who lived in the desert and sought to embrace the Law according to Moses. Its members appeared to dwell in perfect harmony with both heaven and Earth, enjoyed perfect health and lived longer than ordinary men. They healed the sick, taught the ignorant and radiated holiness to all who met them. Their earthly requirements seemed modest; they ate the fruit of the date palm and herbs from their gardens, and communed daily with the holy angels and with God.

Armed with the evidence he had gathered through his research on St. Benedict and St. Jerome, the young Bordeaux went to Monsignor Mercati and asked for permission to enter the Secret Archives of the Vatican. With monsignor's permission, Professor gained entrance into the vitrines in the Scriptorium and subsequently discovered the *Lost Jesus Scroll*. These teachings referred to a man named Jesus, and pertained to his mysterious Invocations of the Angels of the Earthly Mother and the Angels of the Heavenly Father.

Although I took the necessary time to peruse Professor Bordeaux's eighty books pertaining to the Essenes and their customs, and asked Professor many questions about the mysterious *Lost Jesus Scroll*, I was unable to obtain an unedited and unmodified copy of the Vatican document. Apparently there was none. Professor Bordeaux had instead chosen to privately present his translation of the Vatican manuscript in a beautiful and almost poetic form, which also included a number of fragments from the Psalms of David.

In spite of these circumstances and my complete satisfaction that the Lost Jesus Scroll was authentic, I still felt I could not present it to the public without Vatican acknowledgment. Finally, in 1985, I wrote to Pope John Paul II and asked that the authenticity of the ancient manuscript be confirmed. I explained that I felt it imperative that this remarkable work be made available to the world.

Later, that same year, I received news that an announcement of a reading of the Lost Scroll had been made over Vatican radio in the presence of Mr. Mario Spinelli, then a Vatican journalist. Mr. Spinelli reported, without reservation, that the Vatican acknowledged this timeless *message of the Lord*.

Although this was a step in the right direction, I was still not satisfied. I wanted an exact translation of the gospel text, free of any modification and editing. Therefore, I again wrote to Pope John Paul II, asking him to allow one of his own experts in Hebrew and Aramaic to create a direct and unedited translation. I promised faithfully that both the translator, as well as the Vatican, would receive full credit when I presented the Lost Jesus Scroll to the world.

In December 1986 I received the following letter from the Secretary of the Roman Vatican dated December 12th, stating:

> *I am writing to acknowledge the letter which you addressed to His Holiness Pope John Paul II. The sentiments which prompted you to write are appreciated, but I regret that it is not possible to comply with your request.*
>
> *I have pleasure in informing you that His Holiness invokes upon you God's abundant blessings. Sincerely yours, Monsignor G.B.Re, Assessor.*

It appeared that my hope of obtaining an unaltered translation of the Lost Jesus Scroll was now shattered.

Twenty years have passed since first coming in contact with the *Lost Scroll*, although I have continued to work with it. In that the process of transformation rests within the potentiality of every individual, I feel I can no longer wait to present this material. Jesus' practices and teachings regarding utilization of the powerful currents of natural and cosmic law will forever change the lives of those who venture through the open doorway of possibility.

In presenting this remarkable work I have done my best to remove the poetic aspects of Professor Bordeaux's translation, as well as any superfluous scripture, in an effort to correlate the *Lost Jesus Scroll* with the original translation. Having dealt with enumerable ancient manuscripts translated from Hebrew and Aramaic, I believe that the forgoing presentation is well within the range of reasonable accuracy.

CHAPTER II

The Essene Secrecy

The Essenes established their Order during the mid to latter part of the third century BC., because they felt that fundamental Judaic precepts and dogma were weakening the teachings of Moses. Thus, a group of those dedicated to maintaining the purity of the Law made a decision to withdraw from secular Jewish religion. Their hope was to restore the original teachings of their great Lawgiver and thereby also restore the Law to the state it had been during the nomadic years of the tribes of Israel.

The Essenes ultimately became a secret order, not because they wanted to adhere to secrecy, but because they sought to isolate themselves from the masses that followed a more fundamental and outer form of the Jewish doctrine. Because the teachings of Moses were of a deep and mystical nature the Essenes knew that the masses, which followed an outer or exoteric teaching, would not understand the deeper truths of their Lawgiver. Therefore the Essenes did not openly reveal the mystical teachings of Moses to the outside world. Because of this secrecy they were extremely misunderstood. The term Essene was derived from the breastplate of the ancient Hebrew High Priest, which was called an Essen, meaning righteous. Therefore, the name of the sect meant *Righteous Ones,* or those who followed the path of righteousness by adhering to the original laws of Moses. The word also had another meaning, which was taken from the word Essence, or the term, Divine Essence, signifying a person or thing set apart from all that is accidental.

When the Dead Sea Scrolls were discovered, there arose quite a controversy over who the actual founder of the Essene Sect, known as the *Teacher of Righteousness,* was. Reference to such a teacher appears at various times throughout the Dead Sea Scrolls, among these, the "Zadokite" Document. Since, the Essenes originated for the explicit purpose of following the teachings of Moses without dogmatic interference, there is a strong likelihood that the Teacher of Righteousness was probably Moses. It is he whom the Essenes followed, and his laws that they sought to implement.

One of the early authorities on this Essene Sect was Joseph ben Matthias, better known to scholars as the Jewish Historian, Flavius Josephus. The son of a priestly family, his rather enterprising life includes being a priest, a general and a prisoner of Rome. Flavius Josephus began his precocious career by adopting an ascetic life under the guidance of Banus, who was an Essene Master. Although he remained only three years under the tutelage of Banus before joining the Pharisees, Josephus appeared to still hold the Essenes in high esteem. While some consider him a renegade, religious scholars still depend on two of Josephus' greater writings, *Antiquities of the Jews* and *The War of the Jews* to clarify Jewish history.

In his *War of the Jews,* Flavius Josephus writes:

> *Moreover an Initiate into the Monastic Community at Qumran swears to communicate their doctrine to no one otherwise than he received them himself; that he will abstain from robbery, and will equally preserve the books belonging to their sect, and the angels.*

It seemed that any who violated these oaths were cast out of the Essene society (Wars of the Jews: Book II: Chapter VIII, V6). Therefore, the secrecy pertaining to the Essene angelology escaped many modern scholars, that is, until the translation of the *Jesus Scroll*. For the most part, scholars have depicted the Essenes as an over-zealous religious group existing in a monastic community known as Qumran, near the Dead Sea. Unfortunately, this paints a rather dark picture of these rather remarkable followers of Moses, who in fact lived by higher personal and spiritual standards than any other sect. Flavius Josephus tells us that they were Jews by birth and that they seemed to have a greater affection for one another than any of the other sects.

The depth of the Essenes' spiritual vision is perhaps expressed best through the following words excerpted from the Dead Sea Scrolls, Manual of Discipline:

Hymn of the Initiates:

Through His mysterious wonder light is come into my heart; mine eye has set its gaze on everlasting things.

A virtue hidden from man, a knowledge and subtle lore concealed from human kind; a fount of righteousness, a reservoir of strength, a wellspring of all glory wherewith no flesh has conversed, except those whom God has bestowed upon them that he has chosen, to possess them forever.

He has given them an inheritance in the lot of the Holy Beings, and joined them in Fellowship with Sons of Heaven, to form one congregation, one single Fellowship, a fabric of holiness, a plant evergreen, for all time to come."

Many of the disciplines which the Essenes imposed upon themselves and upon those who came seeking to join their Order, if implemented today, could improve the quality of life for the human race. To harness and purify the mind would allow mankind to develop the ability to tame the wild beasts and calm the seas.

To adopt a natural healthy diet would encourage longevity and increase the I.Q, allowing humanity to age more slowly and to have fewer illnesses.

The Essenes realized these values and knew that if outsiders, who had not undergone the disciplines of purification, were allowed into the innermost sanctuary of the monastic aspect of the community, dissension would soon follow. Therefore, all who would seek the love and peace of such solitude would first have to earn the right to have it.

Although the Brotherhood rejected pleasure as an evil, it was not because pleasure was actually considered wrong, but rather because its pursuit simply cannot be fulfilled. It is the nature of people to find pleasure in something today, only to be bored with it tomorrow. Therefore, the Essenes considered pleasure one of mankind's greatest enemies—in that it often hampered the true nobility of the soul because it enticed a person into a fascination with the temporal world. For this reason, the Brotherhood dedicated themselves to practices that were for the common good of all. They developed great wisdom, as well as love, patience, kindness, tolerance, and peace. To the Essenes these qualities were the true values of life.

It was therefore natural for the Brotherhood to focus on God. However, their God was not a God of religious separation, but a universal God; omnipresent, omniscient and omnipotent. By developing practices, which enabled them to be centered in such a power, they were able to walk in the human world, yet share in the angelic realms. Their consciousness became submerged in the consciousness of the Creative Principle of the universe, allowing their minds to become enhanced with greater knowledge, strength and understanding.

While the elders of the primary monastery at Qumran represented the foundation of the Essene Community, there were others who went forth as teachers and healers. Many members, who were not privy to the inner circle, lived in towns throughout Israel and Egypt. This made it possible for a member of the organization to travel from place to place without concern over personal needs or necessitates. What one person owned belonged to all and was shared freely among the Brotherhood. Therefore it was not necessary for Essene travelers to carry anything with them, except those things needed to survive from one destination to another.

No member of the Essene sect ever sold to another, but each worked for the good of the whole. Thus the needs of each were met without monetary reimbursement. Because of this, there was no jealousy, or desire to break the peaceful co-existence existing among the Brothers.

The Essenes also took great pains to study the writings of the ancients, and chose out of these those things that which would be considered as an advantage to their souls and bodies. This included the medicinal use of roots and stones. Considering the illiteracy of the times, it is remarkable to note that the Essenes afforded those who dwelled in the monastic community a rather outstanding education. Some eventually served on the Sanhedrin Council, the supreme council of Israel, while others were known for their prophetic abilities, and yet others as scribes, who worked diligently at preserving the ancient teachings of their forefathers.

The health of the Essenes was also exemplary, for their diet was extraordinarily pure. Because of this the vibration of the body was quickened, thereby lessening the intensity of pain and enabling the body to regenerate itself naturally through the utilization of natural forces, such as sun, water and air. This reduced the number of illnesses incurred by members of the Essene Community and increased the restorative functions of the body so that more expedient healing could be experienced. Due to these disciplined practices members of the sect lived unusually long and healthy lives.

The Brotherhood's scientific approach to the utilization of the natural forces of the earth for the sake of bodily regeneration included the food they ate. Their primary diet consisted of bread and one kind of food, such as a single fruit or a single vegetable. Although it is said that they sat *at meat*, there is no indication that members of the Brotherhood ever consumed animal products. At the same time, they were careful to eat only a single food at a sitting. They believed that each fruit and vegetable was comprised of a different vibratory frequency, thereby giving each its own unique taste and form. Because no two vibrations are alike, the Essenes held that variety was not always compatible. They felt that the vibratory differences often created a lack of harmony within the body and brought greater unrest in the mind.

The Brotherhood believed that God created food for the sake of life. Therefore, they paid respect to the Creator by donning white garments, signifying purity and homage to God, before entering the communal dining room to partake of any meals. Upon completion of the meal, they laid aside their pure white garments and again put on their working attire, after which they resumed their daily duties. Each member of the Essene Brotherhood performed their specific trade for the good of the whole, some as cobblers, others as carpenters farmers, and scribes.

The religious aspects of the Brotherhood are also worth mentioning, primarily because they were more devout in their dedication than the Sadducees or Pharisees, and differed greatly in their views on life and death. The Essenes advocated that the body was corruptible and therefore not permanent, but that the soul was immortal and continued forever.

The soul was believed to come from the subtle air, and united to the body as in prison, having been drawn in by its natural enticements or inclinations. When death came, the soul was set free from its imprisonment of flesh and rejoiced as it mounted upward. Therefore, the Essenes encouraged purity and goodliness, knowing that the Law of Cause and Effect was impartial and precise. Good would reap accordingly and bad would draw undesirable consequences.

Following the crucifixion of Jesus, little attention was given to the Essenes until the discovery of the original *Dead Sea Scrolls* half a century ago in a network of caves at Qumran. Archeologists and religious scholars have since tried to piece together and decipher the scrolls. It is likely this work, however, will continue for many decades yet to come, as reconstruction of the smaller fragments of the scrolls will be a painstakingly slow process.

A large number of devout Christians have been concerned that the discovery of the Dead Sea Scrolls might in someway discredit the Bible. For this reason, some biblical scholars have approached the writings with a measure of trepidation and skepticism. The ancient writings have instead, not only authenticated parts of the Old Testament, but have also shed valuable light on some of the elusive mysteries that walked the corridors of early Christianity. The *Dead Sea Scrolls* and the religious movement they depict have in some ways helped to reconstruct the spirited climate of early Christianity. Certainly they have brought some much-needed clarity to the more hidden teachings of John the Beloved and Jesus the Christ, which is verifiable through the discovery of the *Lost Jesus Scroll*.

Although the *Lost Jesus Scroll* is not considered part of the Dead Sea Scrolls, it is one of the ancient books now contained in a special room within the locked corridors of the Secret Archives of the Roman Vatican, and does correlate with the secrecy of the Essene fellowship. The scroll refers to *peace with the Angels*, and these, or similar, invocations were certainly taught by Jesus. For this reason, it is logical to assume that both John and Jesus were familiar with the inner secrets of the Essene sect.

There is no direct evidence to prove that Jesus was affiliated with the Essenes during the latter years of his life, or during the period referred to as his ministry. However, there are historical accounts linking Jesus with the sect from the age of twelve to young manhood, although there is no mention of this in the biblical scriptures. Nonetheless, this should not be objectionable, for there do not appear to be any historical or biblical documents which state that Jesus was actually a carpenter either. Most have assumed that Jesus applied himself to this occupation simply because it was customary for the males of a family to be taught the family trade. It is written, of course, that Joseph, his father, was considered one of the finest carpenters in all of Israel.

Some of the historical accounts indicate that when Jesus' parents discovered him both teaching and being taught in the Holy Temple of Jerusalem at the age of twelve, they were afraid that he had placed his life in danger. There had apparently been a growing concern amongst the Priesthood at the time that Jesus might be the child who had been singled out to become the forthcoming Messiah. Therefore, some discussion had already taken place among a few of the priests regarding the possibility of putting the youth to death. Certainly, Joseph, who was a member of Israel's prestigious religious assembly, the Sanhedrin, (Book of James XV) would have been aware of any such danger and taken great care to protect his son.

There would have been no safer haven for the young Jesus, than the protective custody of the Essenes, the most profound followers of Moses. Although the Elders, or central council, of the Essene Community shunned marriage, it was not uncommon for them to take other people's children who were pliable and considered fit for learning.

If this is so, and there is a measure of evidence to indicate that it is, then Jesus was not only initiated into the teachings of the Essenes, but would have had an excellent academic education by the standards of the world at that time. Jesus would have also had an opportunity to train his youthful body in the utilization of the powerful forces of nature and cosmic law as he grew into manhood. Although his powers were already present when he was sent to the Essenes, administration of the sect's rigid disciplines would have enabled the young Master to more fully control his senses.

Certainly the *Lost Jesus Scroll* reveals a correlation between Jesus and the Essenes, which is based on his knowledge pertaining to the utilization of the natural forces of earth and the powerful currents of cosmic law.

There has been a great deal of skepticism about Jesus' probable affiliation with the Essenes, primarily because of the lack of biblical references. However, neither are there any references as to where Jesus spent his *lost years* (ages one to three, three to twelve and twelve to thirty), primarily because tradition has primarily focused on the resurrection. Unfortunately many who have remained centered on this aspect of Jesus' life do not fully understand or accept that the true heart of Christianity which focuses not only on the resurrection of Jesus, but the resurrection of all mankind. The reason for such oversight could be that those who teach about the forthcoming end of the world did not then, and do not today, fully understand—the personal resurrection.

Understandably, the Essenes did not openly reveal the mystery of their work with the angels to the uninitiated masses. There is, however, reference in the *Manual of Discipline*, a segment of the translated *Dead Sea Scrolls*, as to their existence and at what times these special invocations were to be practiced:

Manual of Discipline, cols, X-XI: I:
Day and night will I offer my praise and at all the appointed times which God has prescribed. When daylight begins its rule, when it reaches its turning point, and when it again withdraws to its appointed abode.

The *Lost Jesus Scroll* describes Jesus' instructions to his closest followers concerning the *Invocation of the Angels*. He taught that they should practice those pertaining to the forces of earth by morning, the forces of peace by noon and the forces of the Heavenly Father by night. He also refers to these powerful forces of Natural and Cosmic Law as *angels,* possibly because illiteracy prevailed and the people of his time could not comprehend a personal utilization of natural and heavenly forces.

In presenting the *Scroll*, the forces of natural and cosmic law are not represented as angels, but powerful forces emanating from God. The primary reason for doing this is to illustrate that each of the Invocations correlate to specific aspects of the Creator. At the same time these forces also collectively represent that one creative Principle which brought forth the universe and which exists in and through all forms of life.

These Invocations of the Angels are just as powerful today as when Jesus taught them to his disciples 2,000 years ago. Any who perseveres and practices them will soon find themselves in a new world, where the flame of their own forthcoming greatness will set fire to new ideas and bring forth a different way of life. Certainly, the Invocations could establish greater peace and harmony, not only to Christianity, but also to the world.

CHAPTER III

Keys to Understanding the Lost Jesus Scroll

Before perusing the *Lost Jesus Scroll* it is important to understand its purpose. Nothing presented in the past, either by the spoken word, or in writing, lays out a procedure for human transformation more beautifully than that which Jesus taught his followers on the shores of Galilee. This process of the *Resurrection of the Dead*, defining the future transformation of mankind, has, in the past, been among the most secret religious teachings throughout history.

With the discovery of the *Scroll*, the path to the resurrection itself is not only clarified, but also establishes a road map toward both inner and outer peace. The traditional belief that the *Battle of Armageddon* will herald the end of the world, as well as a time when all the dead will be called from their graves to gather for a final judgment is quickly replaced by the concept of a personal resurrection, or transformation, and replaces death with an awareness of eternal life.

In view of the many scientific discoveries during the past decades pertaining to creation, it is now necessary to look upon the writings of the ancients and reevaluate their meaning. Did the prophecies of old really speak of a time when our outer world would be destroyed, or did they speak of a time when man would transcend his state of humanness through a process of inner transformation and rise to some higher state of existence? In *St. John's Revelation* there is a definite indication that the end times will not fall upon collective mass consciousness through an outer battle, but upon each individual as they fight for supremacy over that part of their nature which persists in going contrary to the way of the Christ.

It is also apparent, that some of those who closely followed the Master from Galilee were privy to the inner mysteries of the *Resurrection of the Dead*. They knew that there would be a seventh epoch, referred to as a day in the systematic evolutionary progression of earth, when the human race would bring forth a new and enlightened consciousness. John the Beloved describes this transformation in his *Revelation*, when he discloses the three levels of battle that occurs within the soul's divine metamorphosis. These levels were presented first in the form of a great dragon, representing the ego and self will, followed by two beasts, symbolizing the purification of the mind and the purification of the soul. Therefore, one should not be too surprised to discover that John also revealed the process by which this remarkable change could be accomplished. This, in fact, is the very heart of the *Lost Jesus Scroll*.

The mysteries revealed in the *Scroll* have their roots firmly embedded in the teachings of Moses. The great Lawgiver, like the notable teachers before him, and those who came later, also taught two distinct teachings. One teaching is presented to the people in terms of many simple Laws, which were but a shadow of Moses' deeper instruction. Unfortunately, because the life and deeper teachings of the great Hebrew master are so massive and would fill an entire book, only a few highlights will be included here.

These will consist of those teachings ultimately incorporated into the Essene teachings, and later as they appear in the *Lost Jesus Scroll*.

Moses was called up the mountain to meet with God in the quiet solitude of the Sinai Peninsula. There he began the journey of illumination and transformation, which would govern his remaining days on earth. Such a state of ascended consciousness is better known in today's modern world as Cosmic or God Consciousness.

This merger of the finite human mind with the infinite mind of God has not been experienced, or even heard of, by many people in today's world. However, there is irrefutable evidence that this transformation has occurred through the centuries in different people at different times. Scientists, theologians of all traditions, philosophers, composers, and even artists have revealed this remarkable wonder in their writings and paintings. Yet, in every case, the revelation of those who unite with the mind of God is always the same. This is the revelation of all revelations and the prophecy of all prophecies, as it is also the one Law that created the universe. St. John the Beloved describes this resurrection in his *Revelation* as a period when the soul is shaken on its foundation and great revelations descend upon it as lightning.

Although Moses wrote the Ten Commandments as he received them from God and, in turn, gave them to the Children of Israel, these were only the exoteric, or outer, aspects of his teachings. His primary focus was to initiate his followers, particularly the heads of the twelve tribes of Israel, into a deeper comprehension of creation and to reveal God's Divine plan. He also wanted to establish a number of laws that would survive his death in order to leave a basic direction of transformation for his people, and insure that they might possess peace and plenty. Thus, Moses created no law, or built no edifice that did not reveal these mysterious wonders, beginning with the construction of his *Tabernacle in the Wilderness*. Since the *Lost Jesus Scroll* correlates with Moses' delineation of creation, as revealed in his seven prong candlestick, it seems important to begin there.

The Tabernacle consisted of three compartments. These signified the outside court, or body of the people, the Room of the Holies, signifying the soul, and the Holy of the Holies, signifying the Spirit of God, who abides within every soul and gives it existence.

The *Court* represented not only a place for the people to worship, but it was also a symbol of mass consciousness, or those not yet sufficiently developed to enter into the inner sanctum of divine metamorphosis. The *Room of the Holies*, however, as well the third compartment, the *Holy of the Holies*, represented the deeper aspects of Moses' teachings pertaining to those things that were hidden from those in the outer Court. For this reason the two inner compartments were considered sacred and attended only by the high priest and those sanctified to assist him.

The *Room of the Holies* represented the soul and contained a seven-pronged candlestick, an incense burner and twelve loaves of shew-bread arranged in two stacks of six loaves each. Of these symbols, the candlestick was considered the most holy, for it signified God's creation, as well as His Divine Plan.

Moses' understanding of God and God's Divine Plan originated when he saw the burning bush during his first ascent of Mt. Sinai. While observing the bush, which did not burn at touch, Moses perceived it as the consciousness of God flowing through all form, from vegetation to human. Later this inspired the seven-pronged candlestick, which was cast in gold to signify the spirit and wisdom of God, as well as the seven epochs of creative progression.

Several centuries after Moses death, the Essenes took the symbolism of the seven pronged candlestick and applied it to their *Tree of Life*. This was later revealed by Jesus in the *Lost Jesus Scroll* under his *Invocation of the Angels*.

The following is an outline of the symbolism of Moses' seven-pronged candlestick, as translated from original Hebrew.

First Epoch – Day One: And God brought forth the Light and made a division between the light (intellectual elementizing) and darkness (not manifested all knitting).

Second Epoch – Day Two: God affected a separation between the waters that were below and waters that were above. From that time there was east-dawn, the Light of the Consciousness (Heaven) and west-eve, the dark, meaning not yet manifested potential (Earth).

Third Epoch – Day Three: To the dark non-manifested earth he assigned the gathering place of the waters, or seas. And to the earth he assigned growing grass, vegetable substance and fructuous, yielding-fruit. Each would reproduce after its kind.

Fourth Epoch – Day Four: And the Light of Consciousness was given the symbolic representation of day, and that part of it which became cloaked in matter, yet created from the light became the representation of eve, or unknowing.

Fifth Epoch – Day Five: Came wormlike soul-of-life trailing along and swimming, fowl flying above the earth and huge hulked bodies. Each reproduced after its kind and multiplied the earth.

Sixth Epoch – Day Six: And He made the quadruped-existence. He made Adam, universal man, the collective unity of all human existence, both male and female. These would become an outer shadow, or expression, of the Divine Plan.

Seventh Epoch – Day Seven: On the Seventh Day God re-established himself on earth and restored the world. (Thus, God would come forth in all mankind and His consciousness would then prevail over earth. When this has come to pass human will no longer be human but divine. This would become known, or called, the end time, or the end of human existence as it is known today.)

The measurements of the *Ark of the Covenant* were also very precise and symbolically configured to signify the metamorphosis of the soul as it came before the throne of indwelling God, or the *Law*.

Great pillars stood at the entrance of the tabernacle signifying the four elements binding the soul to matter. In order to proceed to the inner world, or inner rooms, it would be necessary for the soul to free itself from its worldly attraction and earthly desires.

The *Tabernacle in the Wilderness* tells the story of humanity's bondage to matter. Only through purification of the corporeal desires (laver of water) and purification of the harmful patterns the soul incurs during its journey through matter (altar of fire), could the soul enter into the *Room of the Holy*, which contained the mystery of the seven epochs of creation.

Along with the seven-pronged candlestick, twelve loaves of shew-bread had also been placed in the *Room of the Holies*. These were separated into two stacks of six to delineate Earth's current state of progression. The shew-bread was arranged in such a manner as to show that the spiritual nature mankind was bound to the sixth, or human, cycle of progression, as was the soul. These two selves (unleavened bread in stacks of six) could only free themselves by returning to the One (1-2).

The two consciousnesses, thus united, could then enter of the *Holy of the Holies*, representing the indwelling Spirit of God within every soul, and open the *Ark of the Covenant* containing the *Law of God*.

The forgoing is but an infinitesimal part of the massive symbolism Moses left behind, but it bears witness to the same mysteries St. John the Beloved wrote in his *Revelation* centuries later. It also established a framework for the *Tree of Life*, the central focal point of the Essenes.

The *Tree of Life* used by the Essenes was a symbolic representation of Moses' seven-pronged candlestick. At the same time it also outlined a process by which mankind could accomplish the

Great Work, or the metamorphosis of human to divine through the utilization of seven cosmic forces and seven natural forces. These formed the foundation of the Essene's relationship with the Angels, which later became such an integral part of the *Lost Jesus Scroll*.

CHAPTER IV

The Essene Code of the Angels

Clearly the Essenes realized the significance of Moses' *Tabernacle in the Wilderness*. In what has become known as the *Dead Sea Scriptures*, the Brotherhood referred to the approaching transformation of humanity a number of times, but it is particularly expressed in their *Tree of Life*.

The *Tree of Life* is even more ancient than the Essenes and dates as far back as King David, (Proverbs 3:18). Nonetheless it did not become a representation of creation and its eternal progression until the Essene era. Obviously, the Essenes realized that Moses' candlestick symbolized seven epochs, or seven phases of earth's progression. Because a tree has its roots implanted securely in the earth, yet its branches reach toward heaven, the ancient Brotherhood by the Dead Sea recognized that man was of like nature. They saw man's body as derived from earth and his soul derived from heaven, and that the soul was created in God's image. Accordingly, the Brotherhood correlated their angelology to signify the precise process by which creation came into being. Next, they formulated certain practices to utilize the creative forces of Natural and Cosmic Law, knowing that these would help people to ascend into the final phase of human progression, or the seventh epoch when human becomes divine.

Like Moses, the Essenes observed the Sabbath on Saturday, signifying the day heaven and earth would become one and human was no longer human. Thus, the Sabbath was considered the most holy day of the week and set aside as a day to pay homage to God, who is not only the Spirit of the Universe, but who will ultimately become manifest in all human beings.

There were twenty-one Invocations. The first seven were relegated to morning worship and performed in the first part of the day. These were associated with the sun, water, air, life, health, joy and oneness with earth. The next seven were associated with peace and were practiced at high noon when the sun was high in the sky. These were comprised of peace with the body; peace with the mind; peace with the family; peace with humanity; peace with culture; peace with earth and peace with the Heavenly Father.

The seven final Invocations were considered holy and sacred to God alone. Because God had brought forth creation from unmanifested darkness, evening worship was relegated to the invisible heavenly forces. These included power, love, wisdom, eternal life, creative work, peace and oneness with God.

Performed in the proper sequence the Invocations not only revealed the sequential order of the seven epochs of creation, but also a method by which every human could enter into the union with earth and heaven and thereby complete their journey through matter. Thus, the world would not end in the fire of war and destruction, but in the fire of soul purification, when human life would be purged of its corporeal tendencies and take upon itself a semi-light or semi-material body of higher form.

Apparently the Essenes felt that it was impossible for any one individual to utilize and practice all twenty-one of the natural and cosmic forces every day. Therefore, the primary Invocations were assigned days of the week and practiced each evening and each morning, while the seven pathways to peace were reserved for high noon. This division made it possible to complete all twenty-one Invocations within a seven-day period.

Because the forces of nature were considered a mere reflection of the heavenly forces, it was customary to begin the evening with the Invocation of the angels representing the cosmic forces. These were then followed on the subsequent morning with the Invocations of its shadow, or the physical manifestation overshadowing the invisible forces. In time, as the cycles were repeated, the soul not only learned to incorporate all of the natural and cosmic laws in day-to-day living, but to also overcome its affinity for earth. Once it had united with its indwelling divine counterpart, the soul was considered to have *raised the dead* (raised the God, or Christ Self from its entombment of matter) and no longer imprisoned by worldly ways.

A more detailed explanation of the personal fellowship the Essenes had with these forces of natural and cosmic law would not be possible if it were not for the *Lost Jesus Scroll*. In the scroll, John the Beloved presents Jesus' teachings relating to each one of the natural and cosmic forces separately. Obviously, Jesus not only taught the specific Invocations applicable to each angel, but he also explained the utilization of each force and the effect each might have on the body, the mind and the soul.

With the background of the *Lost Jesus Scroll* established, it will be easier for the reader to understand and utilize the practices as they appear in the following pages. It is well to state here, that reading alone cannot develop the powers as they are presented in the scroll. This requires dedicated practice. For those who decide to participate wholeheartedly in the adventure, however, the rewards are greater than they can possibly imagine.

The Lost Jesus Scroll

Section One

MYSTERIES OF THE FORCES OF EARTH

SECTION ONE

CHAPTER ONE

Son of Heaven – Son of Earth

Israel, its name means *having power with God,* possesses a gracious beauty that lives high in its tallest mountains and falls silent in its lowest plains. To those accustomed to the mad rush of modern civilization, it might seem barren and remote. Yet, to the millions who come to see the land where Jesus of Galilee once walked, there is a certain elegance, silence and peace.

Israel has changed a great deal since Jesus taught his followers, for its cities have been captured in the forward thrust of time and have become quite modern. Therefore, experiencing the old Israel is not easy and can be accomplished only through the study of Israel's history and maps of its ancient past.

The Hebrew year begins in Nisan, or A'bib, the time of the Spring Equinox. The melting snows of Lebanon fill the Jordan channel in some places and the river overflows. Even as the barley is harvested in Jericho and the Jordan, the uplands are covered with brilliant vegetation and flowers. By June and July, the months of Tammuz, the country of Judea becomes a dreary wasteland of withered stalks and burned grass. The heat is intense and continues its rule until the rains again soften the ground during the thirty-day reign of Ethanim, September and October. At that time the Holy Land succumbs to winter, and during the month of Tebeth, December and January, the flocks leave the highlands for the Jordan Valley. Rain, hail and snow garnish the higher hills, occasionally falling upon the Queen City, Jerusalem.

In all of Israel there were two places Jesus loved most, his beloved Capernaum by the shores of Galilee and the Garden of Gethsemane.

The City of Capernaum rests on the northern shore of the Sea of Galilee. Once it had its own synagogue, built by the Centurion and a detachment of Roman soldiers garrisoned there. In the ancient days there was also a customs station, where the dues were gathered both by stationary and itinerant. However, it was not these things that drew Jesus to Capernaum, but its natural beauty. He found solace in the quietude of the groves that lined the banks of the Sea of Galilee. By day the sun cast its heat across the cool water, while on a moonlit night the water was bathed in silver. It was here that the brothers, Simon Peter and Andrew, received a call to become Jesus' disciples.

Capernaum, also known as the town of Nahum, was not actually one of Jesus' residences, as some believe, although he spent a great deal of time there. Jesus simply found delight in coming to the sea and sitting with his followers in the early morning sunrise and the evening sunset. Other times, when winter fell upon the land, Jesus frequented the home of Peter, and usually one or more of his disciples gathered with him to listen to his teachings.

Some distance away was the Garden of Gethsemane, the other place Jesus often frequented. Resting on the outskirts of Jerusalem, it offered a sharp contrast to Capernaum. Still Jesus found much peace amid the olive trees standing at the base of the Mount of Olives. It was a private place. Sometimes he came to sit beneath one of the trees to be alone and commune with God in the silence of his heart. Other times he came with his disciples and taught.

About a mile and a half from Jerusalem was Bethany, a village situated on the eastern slopes of Mt. Olivet. This was sometimes referred to as the *House of Misery* because of its lonely situation and the sick and ill who gathered there. It was also the home of Lazarus and his sisters. Many times, when Jesus came to teach at the Temple of Jerusalem, or after seeking the solitude of Gethsemane, he would travel the short distance to dine with them, for he loved the family of Lazarus deeply.

Members of Jesus' blood family also lived near Jerusalem and he was made welcome in their homes as well. Elisabeth, mother of John the Baptist and wife of the murdered Zacharias, a priest of the division of Abijan, was the one of the people Jesus often frequented. Although Zacharias had been murdered prior to Jesus' ministry, Elisabeth still lived in their ancestral home located about seven miles out of Jerusalem near the hill country. And, some distance from there was Bethlehem, Judea, a city overlooking the main highway to Hebron and Egypt. This held many remnants of Jesus' past for it included the ancestral home of Anna, wife of the deceased sheepherder, Joachim, and mother of Mary, Jesus' mother.

During the years of his nomadic ministry Jesus remained near the Jordan River much of the time, which was a twisting serpent running through the barren desert land. This was of particular importance in the warmer weather, for the river provided Jesus and his disciples with cool protection from the summer heat and fellowship with the powerful force of water. It was here, along the banks of the Jordan, Jesus often brought the sick and tended to those who came to him for healing. Although he frequently healed by performing miracles, on other occasions he taught his followers to utilize the healing properties the sun, water and air.

"When each has reached that Light, which is brighter than the earthly sun, then shall they be taught by God's angels and come to dwell in His kingdom on earth and in heaven."

Section One

Chapter Two

The Mysteries of Nature

The *Lost Jesus Scroll* opens with the following lines:

One day the sick and maimed came to the mouth of the Jordan where Jesus was teaching. It was in the month of Sivan (May and June). The air was still and the land brilliantly clear, as the parching wind blew from the southern deserts. Wheat harvest had begun in the uplands, the almonds and grapes were ripening, and honey was being collected from the Jordan Valley.

The people came to Jesus, saying, "Master, we are ill and we do not understand why we must suffer in this way, when other people are well. Please help us also become well, for we know you have the power to heal all afflictions."

And Jesus, seating himself amongst them, spoke quietly, but with authority, "You are ill because you cannot understand the ways of heaven and earth. You have transgressed both the laws of God and of nature, although you have done so because unknowing blinds your eyes. Now I will teach you the ways of heaven and earth, and illness will flee from you as vapor rises from the river.

"I tell you truly, your bodies are comprised from the substances of this earth upon which we live. Know you not, Earth is like a mother, and as a mother she tends to the needs of your bodies. As we turned to our mothers by blood when we were but children, we must now turn toward the Holy earth and learn to live in harmony with her ways.

To understand earth and to live according to her ways is to create a body free of disease.

"Even as a river flows into the sea and then rises as vapor to nourish the mountains with rain and snow, so too shall the river replenish the cells of our bodies and purify our blood stream.

"In the spring the snows melt and bring new life to all of the rivers and streams. As we drink plentifully from these rivers and streams, and from the holding vessels that gather the rain in preparation of the hot summer, we are also replenished.

"Even as the water is increased by its exposure to the sun and air, our bodies are also increased by the same holy forces and our bloodstream becomes pure.

"Believe me when I say that the heart is like a mighty sea and gives life to the whole body. The blood that flows through us comes from the sun, the water, the air and the body of our Holy Mother, for each has been brought into being by a loving God that there might be life.

"And as the water must partake of the sun and air to replenish itself, so must man turn toward the sun and air, to renew all that is within and all that is without."

For a moment Jesus paused and allowed his eyes to fall away from the people. It was as though he saw something others could not see and visited where others could not visit. Then he looked again upon those who abided with him and began to speak once more, saying, "Truly, like must be drawn of its nature unto like, and the two shall become one and all things become more powerful.

"When man turns toward those things that bring life to all creation, so shall his body be renewed and made strong, for he shall be like unto the earth and one with all things that live, even the flowers, the trees and the sea.

"Even as water is purified when it flows over the rocks in its journey to a greater sea, so too is the air we breathe purified as it flows across the desert and sings to us through the movement of the trees. It is made strong by mingling with the flowers and the herb-yielding seed, and dancing through the fields of barley and wheat.

"As we draw each breath we draw also from the life which the air has gathered unto it. Although we see it naught, nor do we always smell it, know ye; that to breathe is to breathe not only air, but also all that it contains.

This is possible because earth is a reflection of heaven and moves according to the plan of God."

One of those who followed Jesus and had now come to hear him, asked, "Why then is it necessary that we sit at meat? Would it not be better for us if we did not partake of food?"

"Fasting is sometimes beneficial to the body," Jesus replied. "Even so, if we lived upon nothing but water and air, in time our bodies would become weak, for our bones are made strong by the earth.

"It is our Holy Mother that gives life to all growing things and it is she who nourishes us through the food we eat. And as she has made the grain to stand tall and the flowering tree to bear fruit, so too shall your body become strong when you partake of those grains and fruit she has brought to ripeness.

"If you are to possess a healthy body and healthy mind you must seek oneness with the Earth. You must unite with her forces, for these are the elements from whence your body came into being."

And one who sat with Jesus spoke up saying, "Master, I can see the flow of the water and movement of the trees when the wind blows, but I do not understand you when you say that the earth is like unto our mother."

Jesus smiled when he heard the man's question. He knew that few were those who could look upon the earth as a mother, for they saw only through human eyes and not through the eyes of the spirit. Thus, he replied kindly, saying, "Know that earth is like unto heaven in all things, for she reflects the will of the Heavenly Father. Through her, the flowers bloom, the river flows and the grains grow. If she were not living, then these things could not be. Neither would we have a body to house our soul.

"Learn, therefore, to live in harmony with the laws of our mother and you will have a longer life, less pain, age slower and exist without illness.

"It is lack of harmony that causes mankind to become old and sick, and oft times bring an early and painful death. Nonetheless your transgressions against earth have been done because your eyes cannot see and your ears cannot hear. I tell you truly, this earth is a living plant created within God and therefore an expression of his Holy Law."

"If this be true," another said, "Then how can Satan exist?"

"Your Satan is part of you," Jesus replied, "that part of you bound by sense gratification and the beauty of those things that cause you pain and death. Everything your eye beholds on earth and in the stars is changeable, yet you seek houses that may be destroyed by floods and fire, and possessions that may be stolen, or destroyed.

"Although you love, you seek to possess love and suffer grievously when love passes you by, or death takes it from you.

"Know you, that many suffer illnesses because of their desire for the riches of food and drink. Only death can come from that which is dead.

"And the mind becomes an empty storehouse, because strong drink clouds the senses and causes one to act in all manner of foolishness. They see naught but barrenness when they walk with death as their companion, for that which is dead can bring only disease and pain.

"No man can serve two masters. For either he serves death and all its sorrows, or God and all his angels. Happy are those who follow the way of life, for then you shall know not the plagues that walk with death."

The Mysteries of Nature

And those who had sat with Jesus through the hours and listened to his words knew that his words were true. They also knew that Jesus was like unto no one they had ever seen or heard, for he taught not as the Scribes and Pharisees.

SECTION ONE

CHAPTER THREE

Man Cannot Serve Two Masters

One day Jesus returned to the river's edge that he might again teach the people. At first no one spoke, for Jesus was someone who was holy and someone who could talk to God. After he had seated himself, however, he blessed the people and asked whereof they were troubled.

Then one spoke up asking, "Master, tell us those things that will lead us to the Kingdom of Heaven and tell us also those things we should depart from."

And Jesus replied, "I tell you truly, happiness and nobility must be created in your soul, for it alone is all that you take with you from this world. While your body is mortal your soul is immortal. Everything that exists on earth and in the universe around you is temporal and not within your power.

"You cannot stop the changes upon earth, or the movement of the stars, or halt the coming of death. All these are contained within a power that extends beyond even the universe itself.

"Why grieve then over that which is not yours and cling to which makes you sorrow, or that which makes you ill. Why do you not seek the way of the Heavenly Kingdom? Then heaven can come upon the whole of earth and you will live without want and dwell in harmony. Fear shall flee from you and you shall dwell within the Light of God, which is brighter than even a thousand suns.

"To fear those things that have not yet fallen upon you is to become a slave, for day unto day is sufficient unto itself. True happiness comes from knowing that which is yours and that which belongs to another, for only that which is within you is yours. All other things are temporal and belong to the world.

"But Master," one man cried out. We must eat and we must sleep, for when we hunger there is pain and when we lose a loved one we grieve. How then is it possible for us to find happiness without these things?"

"Is it not within your power to treat all things that befall you, whether good, or evil, with understanding and learning?" Jesus replied. "It is. Therefore, whatsoever be your allocation with life let it be for your learning. On the morrow, what was sorrow today will become joy.

"I tell you truly, wisdom does not come without a price. No man can serve two masters. You cannot have the riches of the world and also possess the Kingdom of Heaven. You cannot desire great lands and possess power over others and also enter the kingdom.

"Know you not, that nothing is given, nor is it had for nothing. In the world of men and angels there is a price."

For a moment Jesus paused, as though to enjoy the beauty that surrounded him. While he was thus quiet, one of his disciples spoke, asking, "Master, who then can enter the Kingdom of Heaven, for have we not all been guilty of seeking the pleasures of earth?"

And Jesus looked upon his disciple John and said, "As you have been forgiven many times for your wrongdoings by your father by blood, so too does your Heavenly Father forgive you a thousand times more.

"You are like little children who go out to harvest a field before the harvest is ripe. Then there is no grain for winter. But as little children you grow into manhood and learn to harvest when the grain is ripe.

"Now the time has come when you must return to your Heavenly Father and become gatherers in his field, for the grain is ripe on the vine.

"I tell you truly, when man has two masters, he will hate the one and love the other, for you cannot serve God and also serve the world. No One can sell you that which they do not own, and none can own that which already belongs to all. This wide earth is yours, and all men are your brothers. There is no need for the son of a king to covet a bauble in the market place."

As Jesus taught a soft glow seemed to emanate about him, and at times it seemed to intensify when he spoke of God and the Kingdom of God. For as he was one with God so did he desire that all should become one. Now, as he spoke of this kingdom, his eyes shone with glory.

"Take then your place at the table of the celebration, and fulfill your inheritance with honor. For in God we live and move and have our being. In truth we are his children and he is our Father.

"He only is free who lives as he desires to live, who is not hindered in his acts, and whose desires attain their ends. He who is not restrained is free, but he who can be restrained or hindered, that man is surely a slave.

"My children, let not the things which are not yours cleave to you! Let not the world grow unto you, as the creeping vine grows fast to the oak, for you will only suffer pain when it is torn from you.

"Naked you came from the womb of your mother by blood, and naked you shall return thither. The world gives and the world takes away. But no power in heaven or earth, can take the Holy Law that resides within you.

"You may see your parents slain, and you may be driven from your country, but go you with a cheerful heart to live in another and look with pity upon the slayer of your parents. Know that by the very deed does he slay himself.

Your true parents are your Heavenly Father and this Holy Earth where we now sit. Death can never separate you from your true parents, and from your true country there is no exile. And within you is the rock that stands against all storms, the Holy Law."

SECTION ONE

CHAPTER FOUR

Three Paths of Purification

And those who had gathered with Jesus at the mouth of the El Urdan (Jordan) sat quietly in the stillness of the day and listened to his words. Then a man spoke, asking, "Master, we know that you speak words of great wisdom, but we are mortal. Can you not teach us the ways of heaven, that we may overcome these grievous illnesses and also the pain within our hearts?"

The Master looked upon the people with tenderness, for he understood their weakness and their sorrows. After thinking for a moment, he replied, "I am happy that you wish to learn those things that few people ever learn, or know.

"Few are the ears that seek the mouth of wisdom and even less those who live by wisdom's dictates. Yet, the path of wisdom is as sweet honey upon dry bread and rain upon a parched land. Because you have asked I shall impart to you those things that so often fall upon ears that are deaf and hearts that are arid and dry.

"Three are the places in you that you must purify. The first is your body, the second is your mind and the third is your soul. In your body are those things that bring illness, old age and death.

"In your mind, which feeds the body, are those thoughts that breed hatred and war. It is your thoughts that leave you as a barren field whose crops have been torn out by a wanton wind, or a river that rises above its banks and floods the valley, leaving in its wake only death and destruction.

"In your soul rests the root of your weaknesses. These feed upon your mind as a stream feeds the sea. It is these that drive you to do those things that bind you to the sorrows of earth"

Jesus paused a moment as though to gather his thoughts, for the words that he would speak could not be understood by many. He sought simple terms that could be expressed in simple language, which all could understand. Shortly thereafter he began speaking again

"Know you, that it is necessary for you to first purify the body, for your body is naught but a vibration of light, sufficiently dense that you can see, feel and sense. Nonetheless the light is dark, not because it is dense, but because it contains impurities that have filled its holy waters.

"Your body is not only light, but it is also water. I would that you know that the body is nourished by the sun, that sun which is even now shining down upon you, and it is sustained by the rivers and streams from whence you drink.

"It is a law that unity draws all things unto its kind, water to water, sun to sun, evil to evil and good to good. Thus your bodies become what you eat, even as your minds become what you think. Put then into your bodies only that, which is supplied by the living earth.

"Eat from the trees that stand strong in the wind, for their fruit will purify and regenerate your body, even as the grain moving in graceful mime will make you subtle and strong.

"Drink of the water that your blood stream runs pure as the river, and bask in the sunlight that the power of earth enter your body and give you strength."

By this time the sun was setting and the water was bathed with color because of its passing, but those who had come to join Jesus did not wish to leave. He possessed power and his words were as magic. They fell softly upon the ears of those around him, like notes of melodious music, even as the lapping waves gently touched the shore.

SECTION ONE

CHAPTER FIVE

The One Law

One day when Jesus was speaking someone asked about the Law, for they were Jews who sought to follow the teachings of Moses through the writings of their holy scriptures. Although Jesus knew well the Law as it was taught to the people, he had also witnessed its fallacy because of misinterpretation. The Scribes, Pharisees and Sadducees argued amongst themselves over who was right and who was wrong. Even among the priesthood, interpretation of the law provoked jealousy and controversy and it was they who sought to control the people. Therefore it was difficult to understand what was right and what was wrong, when even those who taught were of such diverse opinions.

Jesus replied to these questions presented to him by the people regarding the Law, saying, "It is not necessary for you to seek the holy writings in a book to know the Law, as it is all around you. The water reveals its glory through its' powerful seas and in its' rain, for it gathers itself from the ocean crest and rises as mist, to fall again in droplets that sustain and feed all growing things.

"A mountain draws the water unto itself and freezes it into crystals that they might melt in the spring and bring new life to the river. And the tree stands tall and strong, protecting all that seeks its shelter.

"The sun spreads its light over the entire land and gives of itself to every living thing, whether it is a flower, a river, or a tiny child playing by the river's edge.

"If you would but know it, this is the power of God, for he loves all of his people. He cares not whether one is a Jew, or one is a Gentile, nor what color their skin is, or whether one is rich or poor.

"His spirit contains the unnumbered stars, this holy land upon which we walk and yea, even our souls. Therefore His Law is visible in all living things and is everywhere around you.

"The flower teaches us beauty and diversification, even as it as clings to earth and is nourished by the air, water and sun.

"You must take also from the life of the earth and unite with the holy forces of air, water and sunlight. To do so is to become strong in body and swift of foot.

"Flow as the water in the river, yet moving always toward your Heavenly Father, even as the river seeks the sea. Then you shall not become as the stagnant pool, which travels nowhere and becomes filled with all manner of abominations."

One of Jesus' disciples spoke up asking, "Master, how is possible for those who cannot read or write to learn, other than to attend those who are versed in the Law? It is only in such a manner that all people can learn the teachings of Moses."

And Jesus looked upon the disciple, nodding his head. "What you say is true. Yet, those who interpret the law for the people are oft times blinded by their own concepts. Those who follow can rise no further than he who leads.

"Truly, those who seek only the Law in books oft times becomes like an unmoving pool of water, for they allow nothing new into their bodies, their minds, or their souls. In time they become rigid and fixed, dissatisfied with life and intolerant of those who are different than they. Know you not, that they become unhappy with their lot, for they have truly died even before the earth claims their bodies.

"God is Lord of all you survey. He was in the beginning and in the beginning he created all things that were to come, even your own souls. I tell you truly none is more holy than the son of man, for earth is the mother of the son of man. She raises him as a child and prepares him to walk in the garden of the Heavenly father, for only the son of man can become a Son of God.

"Therefore, seek the Law in your own body, your mind and your soul, for when you know yourself so shall you know all beings. In time you shall become as an angel and fly toward the distant stars, where all things are Light.

"First purify you body by eating of those things that the Holy earth provides. Purify your mind by following the in the paths of the great ones who have lived before and purify your soul by performing good works for the sake of all mankind.

"Become therefore a reflection of your Heavenly Father on earth, that all your deeds may shine as a light on a dark night and make better the lives of those who are yet blind. Then you shall become as the husbandman who sowed his grain in the fertile earth and not upon the rock and sand.

"Great is the wheat harvest sown in rich soil, yet greater still is the harvest of a soul, which has sown the kingdom of heaven on earth"

On hearing the wisdom of Jesus the people looked upon him as they might look upon the beauty of a rare jewel. Still they hungered to hear more of those things, which were taught not by the Scribes and Pharisees. And they wished the Master not to depart from them even though the evening was fast approaching.

By this time the sun had set and night was encroaching upon the light of day. Jesus knew that those who had come to be with him now hungered and had need to return to their homes, so he bid them farewell. Rising to his feet, he turned away from them and with his disciples, slowly departing in the deepening dusk.

SECTION ONE

CHAPTER SIX

Natural Healing

On the following day the Master came again with some of his disciples to that place where the forces of the Heavenly Father gathered and the water moved in rhythm as it joined the sea. And again the people came unto Jesus, asking that he teach them about those things that would heal their bodies, their minds and their souls.

Jesus looked upon them with gentleness, and then he sat down among them once more, saying, "It is within your power to merge with the Holy Light of the Heavenly. You must purify your body and your mind that the Holy Light may enter and abide with you forever.

"You who have illness need go to the bank of this river and fast that any uncleanness in you may depart. Join with the water that your body might be washed, and breathe deeply of the air that you might gather strength.

"If you have no illness, it is well for you return to your homes and cease partaking of things that bring diseases to the body. Let your food consist of rich growing grain from the distant hills, fresh fruit and nuts from the trees, and the things you plant, for these are nourished by the soil of the Earth.

"In time you will feel all weakness flee from your body, and even your mind will cease being like unto that of the horse running rampant because it has no master. And it will come to pass that your injuries will heal themselves and you shall become easy of breath.

"I will teach you how to have fellowship with the sun, water and air, for it is possible to become one with each of these powerful forces. Then you will increase the regeneration of your body, the purification of your blood stream and quickly transmute whatever impurities that may dwell within you."

As Jesus spoke, he motioned to those who were seated further away from him, "Come," he said, "sit with me that you might raise your faces to the sun. Through the sun we see the expression and power of our Heavenly Father. Our Holy Earth was born from the Sun and she is a reflection, or shadow, of the Heavenly Father, even as the sun is also a reflection of Him.

"Before earth was, there were untold suns. These were a manifestation of the great Light of the Creator and each carried a part of His Divine Plan within them. I tell you truly, it is possible learn all the mysteries of creation from the sun that now blazes above you."

And it came to pass that some who had joined Jesus did not believe him, for they could not fully understand his wisdom. One man spoke up, scoffing, his voice sharp with ridicule, "How can you say that it is possible to learn the mysteries of creation from the sun? It does not speak. Yet our administrators not only speak, they also think?"

Jesus smiled at the skeptic, for the master was often the target of ridicule and condemnation. Nonetheless, he also felt a sense of compassion, for there were few words to define that which is unspoken. Finally, he spoke, saying, "It is difficult to reveal all things with the spoken word, particularly those things invisible to the human eye. Truly, God is a God of the living and has brought all things into being and all things reflect his nature, if we could but see clearly.

"In such a manner is the sun also living, or it could neither create, nor sustain life. If there was no sun, then there could be no existence; neither would there be plant, animal, or man.

"Know you not, that your bodies are also of the sun. Because it is so, your bodies have a need to be regenerated by the light of the sun.

"Close your eyes and see the sun with the eye of your spirit. Draw your breath inward in slowly and then allow your breath to slowly flow outward.

"As you breath inward, think upon the flower in the center of your body. Therein the light is drawn in and gives you life, even as a flower draws sunlight to itself that it might live and grow.

Allow your breath to depart slowly from you; feeling and seeing the rays of sun fill all parts of your body.

"I tell you truly, you have what no other creature has, for you have the power of reasoning and thought. Thus your power is greater than even that of the sun, which has neither reasoning nor thought. Because this is so, you can direct the force of the sun to any part of your body where illness abides."

And the people did as Jesus taught them. They closed their eyes and began drawing the rays of the sun into their bodies. Soon the inner part of them became hotter than the heat they felt outward and the sun's rays began to course through them like a fire. When they again opened their eyes they felt as though their uncleanness had melted away.

After this Jesus taught them to join in fellowship with the water, saying, "Water holds many keys to life, for it is all giving, even as the sun and air are giving.

"Remember always that each of these forces of earth, and even of heaven, are living expressions of a living God. Therefore, they are holy and must be treated as holy, even as you would worship God - for they are of Him

"Let us sit together here on the river's bank, where the sun, water and air unite."

The people rose and went once more with the Master to the river's edge. Jesus motioned them to be seated and he lowered himself amongst them and began speaking;

"Experience the wonder of the river, for it is more powerful than even the mighty mountains. As it flows over the land it wears away stones and cuts deep crevasses into the hillsides. You must therefore become as the river and learn its ways, and your power will become even greater than the power of the water and you will overcome all things.

"Explain to us Master, how we can become as the water and how this will enable us to overcome all things," one man asked of him.

"It is well that you ask," Jesus replied, "for he who seeks shall find. As all waters flow to the sea so must each seek that path, which will take them to God. To persevere as the river perseveres is to accept each obstacle in life with fortitude.

"To serve all living things as the water serves is to share as co-creators on earth. Then the power of the Heavenly Father becomes your power."

"Close now your eyes and draw the power of the water into your heart, that it might purify your bloodstream. Feel your oneness with the water. See it flow through you, even as it flows across the land."

Silently the people sat, their eyes closed, with the eye of their spirit now focused upon the moving river. In time, they became one with the water and felt its force flow within their bodies. When they again opened their eyes they marveled over what they had experienced and looked upon Jesus with thanksgiving.

When he saw their gratitude Jesus smiled upon them as a father would smile upon a child.

Before departing from the people, Jesus took them once more away from the river's edge and gathered them to him, saying, "Behold all living things require air in order to have life. Only those things that are outside of you breathe according to the law of the

Creator, for you dwell in houses and sleep through the night separated from the holy force of air.

"Each day you should embrace the holy air. Rise therefore in the morning and greet the sun. Let your mind be upon the holy breath that flows through all creation. Feel the energies of the atmosphere flow through your body, as though you were in the center of the distant stars.

"And you shall feel your oneness with all things and the power of the holy air shall increase all of the functions in your body and you shall feel its healing breath.

"I tell you truly, no human being can control the holy forces without the power of breath.

"Even the universe breathes, for on the incoming breath all creation was set into motion and on the outgoing breath all creation became manifest. Between the incoming and outgoing breath are contained the secrets of the universe.

"And when you have learned to share in all of the forces of the earth and have learned the power of love, no ferocious creature, serpentine, or venomous insect that flies shall come nigh upon you."

And the people closed their eyes, listening first to the silence around them. Then they saw the sun through the eye of their spirit. And they felt their unity with the forces of earth and it was as though the power of the earth was within them. And the people felt the healing force of the air to move through their body.

Finally Jesus' followers opened their eyes. Looking around, those who now sat with him saw that the light of day was again fading into the night and the stars were appearing like windows in heaven. They knew that they must leave the master and return to their homes. Some thought this separation painful, for they wanted to learn more of those things Jesus taught.

SECTION ONE

CHAPTER SEVEN

Law of Life

One day Jesus came again to Capernaum, which lay among several cities along the Sea of Galilee. His habit was to visit many of these cities and to teach, with the exception of Tiberius one of the nine larger towns surrounding the sea. Tiberius was situated on the edge of the ancient walled town Rakkath, or Hammath, and a cemetery lay beneath it. For this reason strict Jews usually avoided it. However, Jesus did not frequent Tiberius for another reason - it was noted for its lavishness as a hot-water-bath resort and he had long taught that riches were often a deterrent in one's journey to God.

Generally the master traveled from Jerusalem, along the Jordan River, to the Sea of Galilee, also known as the Sea of Tiberius. From time-to-time he met with those who lived in Magdala, or Magadan, and occasionally even went beyond Capernaum to Chorazin. On this day, however, Jesus remained in Capernaum and as was his customary practice, he made his way to the river's edge with his disciples. It was the month of Tammuz (June/July), and khamassen, a southerly wind was blowing. The heat was intense and the springs and vegetation had dried up. Thus the land was parched, dry and hard; a waste of withered stalks and burnt-up grass.

Jesus sat beneath one of the trees in a nearby grove and his disciples seated themselves nearby. At first they sat quietly, but word had spread concerning Jesus' arrival and soon others came to be with him also. Some came who had been with him at the water's edge when he taught them concerning the Holy Breath. Now they joined his disciples and also sat silently, lest they break the hush of expectancy that seemed to embrace the land.

Finally Jesus opened his mouth and began to teach, saying, "Give thanks to your Heavenly Father, who has instilled healing in the herbs and life in the grains and in the fruit, for those who partake of this wealth shall live long upon the earth.

"You should not kill, for life has been given to all things, both human and animal. Therefore those who kill, kill in part themselves. Long is their suffering and torment, not only in their body, but in their minds and in their souls.

"Know you not, that those who kill for the sake of wanton killing possess violence in their mind. Their minds are filled with hatred and their souls are filled with unrest. The fear that courses through their victims become their fear and the warring nature of the beast enters into their minds, becoming a river of violence that destroys all in its path.

"The Law of our Heavenly Father is just and He sees all things. Only in His service can violence be defeated by peace. Therefore, learn to love and protect all creatures, for where there is love man shall not destroy human or beast."

Then, one man, who had come to be with those who now sat with Jesus, asked, "What should I do, Master, if I should come upon a wild beast in the forest and it is attacking my brother? Am I to allow it to kill a fellow- being, or if I should kill it, would I be transgressing the Law?

And Jesus looked upon the man with a measure of sadness, for man was greater than beast, but nonetheless one would have to live and one would have to die. He spoke quietly, "I tell you truly, of all the creatures upon the earth, man is greater, for he alone was created to bear the image of the Heavenly Father. Therefore you do not transgress the Law if you kill an animal that you might live, or that you might save the life of your fellowman.

"Man is more than beast, but those who kill a beast without just cause, though the beast attacks him not, nor those who are with him, is like unto a beast.

"I say this not only because death and bloodshed have long been the way of man, but because he who wantonly kills human or beast, possesses a violence within him that often erupts and injures all whom he may know.

"As long as violence prevails within the soul, it must express itself accordingly and man, who is more than beast, turns into beast. Wherefore his end is often one of violence and pain. To possess peace is to be at peace with all living things."

Another man, who had been sitting silently, spoke up saying, "Moses, the great leader of our people, allowed our ancestors to sacrifice those beasts that had been made clean. He forbade only unclean beasts. Which then is the Law of God, that of Moses, or your law?"

And Jesus looked upon the man quietly, for the question was one to provoke deep thought. Finally he replied, saying, "Moses received the ten commandments from God when he dwelled in a high place, which few have ever known. Moses knew that the commandments were difficult and that the people would not be able to obey them. When he saw this he was filled with compassion and gave them ten times Ten Commandments, less hard, that they might follow them.

"I tell you truly, had your ancestors been able to obey the ten laws of God; there would have been no need for more. Know you this that he, whose feet are strong as the mountain of Zion, needs no crutches; but he whose limbs do shake gets further having crutches than without them."

"And Moses, feeling that the people would be lost did ask God to suffer him to create other laws, in order that the people not perish. And Moses broke the tablets, which had been given to him by God that your ancestors might live.

"Now the Scribes and Pharisees have made a hundred times the Laws of Moses, which even they cannot obey. Yet they would that you obey them. They have placed upon you a burden that you cannot bear. I say to you, that more the laws of man further are these laws from the Law of God. The Heavenly Father is the one Law, and upon this one Law is based all the laws in heaven and on earth.

"I teach you a simple way, that you might have abundant and healthy lives.

"Both men and beasts were put to death during the days your ancestors walked upon earth. Thus Moses saw the hardness of their hearts and allowed them to sacrifice animals that they might turn away from the killing of their own kind.

"Now I say to you that you should not kill your fellow man, or the beasts that walk upon earth. If you indeed partake of the grain growing on yonder mountainside and the fresh fruit, which makes heavy the branches of a tree, you shall come to dwell in the Garden of Eden, as it was in the beginning."

And those who had come to sit with Jesus beneath the trees near the lake's edge marveled at his words.

"Remember always", Jesus added, "death comes from death and life comes only from life. If, the food that you put into your mouths is a dead food, then it cannot give you life, nor heal your diseases. Yet, if it should be a living food, it will course through your body, purify your blood stream and make strong your bones. It will also heal all manner of diseases."

Another man spoke up, asking, "You speak about life, but what is life? I walk and I breathe, but I do not know what makes this possible.

And Jesus spoke, saying, "Life is like a fire, or a flame, and emanates directly from your Heavenly Father. Moses saw this as he watched the flame which did not burn flow through the thorn bush. He saw it as the fire of life and that it flowed directly from God.

"This flame of life flows pure and unrestrained through all creatures. When this flame is lessoned by that which no longer lives, then an altercation takes place between all that is pure and all that is impure. Little by little the flame of life is extinguished and the body succumbs to sickness, pain and death."

"But how can we prepare our foods without the fire of death? Is that not impossible?" another asked.

Jesus smiled and said, "Eat of those foods that have been grown and ripened by the earth. Grind your grain into fine meal, that it might be mingled with the warm milk of the ewe, or mixed with water from the flowing river and made into fine cakes. Take then the cakes and bake them on the hot stones in the noonday sun, that you are nourished by the water, the air, and the sun, all of which are of the fire of life.

"Eat always from the table of the holy earth. It is spread out all around you if you would but see. She soughs in the trees, flows through the earth and moves joyously through the ripples of the water. To partake of her table is to make pure your body.

"When your body has been made pure, you shall be one with all that lives. You shall be like the trees, strong and stalwart, graceful as the moving grass, and joyful as the river moving toward the mighty sea.

SECTION ONE

CHAPTER EIGHT

Foods in Their Season

The days passed and summer continued to hold the countryside in its embrace. During this time Jesus came again to the people of Capernaum and sat among them and his disciples also.

Speaking to those assembled, Jesus said, "It is wise to eat only twice a day, once when the sun is high in the sky and again when the sun is set.

For all things in the world of man and nature are subject to the cycles of day and night. When the sun is high in the sky the body is hungered, and when the sun sets, the body must face the long hours before it is fed again.

"Therefore, eat when the sun has warmed your food from the chill of the night and again before night comes once more and weakens the strength which day has implanted in it.

"It is also best for you to eat only those foods in season, for then your bodies will be in harmony with the passing months of the year.

"I tell you truly, you will feel the heat less in the summer if you restrain yourself from foods that serve your bodies during the winter. Yet, the rich grain from the fields and the nuts from the trees shall keep you warm when the cold air of the winter touches you.

"To live in harmony with the seasons is to live in harmony with the powerful forces of earth, even the great winds and rain, and yea, even the snows that fall on the distant mountains."

"Master," asked one who was familiar with Jesus, "Tell us what to eat during the seasons of the year, that we might possess the power to overcome the heat and the cold."

Then Jesus spoke again, saying, "It is well that you ask these things, for then you shall be increased in body and mind.

"In the month of Ijar (April-May) eat of the newly harvested barley while it is still filled with life, as it has only recently been severed from the life-force that has fed it.

"But in the month of Sivan (May-June) gather the fresh fruit, that your body may become less. The power of the sun has ripened it to fullness and like the water the juice of the fruit will purify your bloodstream. Then the life force that has been given to the fruit by the air and the sun shall enter into your body.

"In the month of Eluh (August-September) eat the maize growing in your fields and pick the pomegranates as they ripen on the vines. The fruit will purify your bodies and its rind will protect you against the creatures (tapeworms) that oft times inhabit the bodies of those who are unclean.

"In the month of Marcheshvan (October-November) your bodies must increase in preparation against the colder months ahead. Eat therefore of the grains from the fields and pick from the trees laden with sweet dates. Then your bodies shall not feel the chill of the winter.

"In the month of Tebeth (December-January) eat of the grains you have stored, but go then to the orange grove and pluck also its fruit. I tell you truly that this fruit is like unto the sun and will nourish your body and make pure your bloodstream.

"After this partake of the rich herbs, for these shall cleanse and make pure your body in preparation for the heat of the summer.

"Know you not, your bodies are a holy temple that houses the Lord of the Heavens and as you purify your synagogues and temples, it is even greater that you keep pure your bodies and your mind.

"Truly, you should not eat when you are vexed with your neighbor, or angry with your enemy, or even if you sorrow, for all that is within you then becomes sour and turns to poison. That which is poison will destroy your life and your days will be filled with sickness.

"Offer therefore your gifts to the Lord on the altar of your body and remove all impure thoughts from your mind and your life shall be long upon the earth.

After pausing for a time to make certain that those who had come to listen to him understood, Jesus continued. He spoke of the early morning, for long had he relished the rising of the sun above the hills. In watching the light slowly fill the sky, Jesus saw life awaken, and with it the dawn of new beginnings.

Now he chided the people gently, instructing, "And when God sends His sun to awaken you each morning, obey His summons and rise. Sad are those who remain in the abyss beyond wakefulness. They greet not the day in joyous celebration, as they hear not the music of the birds, nor see the opening of the flowers.

"The earth was built in joy, and joy is within the grasp of all people. Yet, those who seek another world because they seek escape from the earth often find it difficult to be happy.

"Do not look upon your daily labors as drudgery, but serve the Lord in all that you do. Know you not, the maiden at the loom and the man at the plow are beautiful in the eyes of the Heavenly Father?

"Those who seek the ways of idleness darken their own hearts, their minds and their souls. They put not their shoulders to the harvest, or serve as guardian over sheep, but oft times steal and plunder and war because they seek not the path of good.

"I tell you truly, when night has fallen across the earth, it is then your Heavenly Father blesses you with rest and covers the heavens with stars."

And Jesus rose from amidst those who sat with him and made his way toward the home of Simon Peter that he might dine there. His disciples rose also and departed with him, for the sun was setting and they also hungered.

SECTION ONE

CHAPTER NINE

Jesus' Seven Pathways to Inner Peace

Once again during month of Tammuz, the month in which the broken tablets of Moses were remembered, Jesus came to rest in the quietude of Capernaum. It was still the summer season in Israel, and even here where the sun, water and air mingled, heat invaded the solitude.

The Master came as he always did, his sandaled feet barely leaving an imprint in the dry soil. Even so, the people gathered to hear his words, for he spoke with the wisdom of the ancients.

"Master," they cried, "We practice those things you have taught us, but still we have no peace. How can we achieve peace?"

When Jesus heard these words he looked upon the people with compassion, for they were like children, and as children they had come to seek comfort from the harshness of daily life. And now he spoke to them with gentleness and yet resolve; for he knew a child needed the firm hand of a father in order to learn to walk.

"Generations have sought peace, even as their hands have

warred. They fight with ignorance because they know neither the laws of earth, nor the laws of heaven. Because people desire those things that are temporal, such as riches and fine clothes, they are never satisfied.

"Know ye not that only those who come to oneness with the Heavenly Father and all that He contains shall know the true feeling of peace.

"Many help not their fellow country men in time of need. They walk past beggars upon the roadway without giving them a drink of water on a hot summer's day. Such is the cruelness in the hearts of those who understand not the laws of heaven and earth. Such people suffer grievous plagues, for their hearts are heavy and their minds full of turmoil because of unfulfilled desires.

"I tell you truly, no one enters the Kingdom of Heaven whose body, feelings, emotions, mind and soul have not been cleansed.

"Your soul and also your body is the temple of the living God and He abides therein. Thus, your soul must be cleansed and garnished, even as you clean your bodies. Then the Lord will reward you with good health and long life."

"But Master," someone spoke out, "How is it that we can purify our souls?"

"Your soul is not your body," Jesus replied, "but rather it houses your body, even as the Heavenly Father houses your soul. Your body will decay one day and return to the earth, but your soul will forever be. Even so, it contains impurities.

"Your soul is like unto a field that was once unplanted and wherein nothing grew. When it was created it was fertile, but had no husbandman to till the soil. One day you left the dark womb of the beginning that you might labor in your field. And as you labored you sowed. In time your crops grew, where before there had been nothing but unplowed earth. So did tares also grow among the grain, and because of this your harvest was lessened. Now the tares must be removed before the grain is ripe so that your harvest will be rich."

"But Master, how did the tares get into our souls and how then can they be removed?" asked another.

"The tares have come into being because of what you have done and what you have thought," Jesus answered. "Thus, you must purify your feelings, your emotions, and your mind, for these are the sources of war and unjust accusations against your neighbors. Man, filled with hatred, despondency and deceit plots against his neighbor and wars to get that which is not his to have.

"In such a manner have the people lived throughout the ages. They will find peace only when they tame the abyss of emptiness that abides within them.

"Therefore when someone asks you for help, hold out a willing hand. To those you hate, give to them from your table, and to those who seek war – turn away, for their ignorance will in the end destroy them. However, do not bear judgment against anyone, for then you will carry also the burden of another's torment within you.

"The Heavenly Father created all things beautiful and only eyes that are blinded more than those of a blind man can see ugliness. Indeed, those who are truly blind may oft times see more of God's glory than those who have eyes that can see. I tell you truly, the blind cannot see the twisted faces of hate and anger, or see the brutal blows one throws upon another.

"All whose souls are filled with hatred and anger must of need live in the ugliness of their own hearts and minds and bodies, and the earth shall be to them a reflection of all that is evil.

"I tell you truly, those who are kind and good, and who have learned to love all people will live in heaven on earth and the earth will be beautiful to their eyes, for it then reflects the true glory of the Heavenly Father.

"Believe me when I say that the world will not end in bloodshed, but in glory, and all shall see it. Wash therefore, not only your body, but also wash the impurities within your mind and soul."

"Oh Master," one of the people spoke, "How can we cleanse our souls and our hearts when all who are around us breed violence and death."

Jesus looked upon them kindly for he knew that man had persecuted man since the beginning. To worship the heaven and the earth was easy, but to walk upon earth as an angel when others walked in ignorance and violence was not easy.

And he spoke to them, saying, "I would have you remember this always; He whose mind possesses all knowledge but whose heart cannot love is as a fire that destroys all in its path, yet sees not nor feels not the cries of its piteous victim. You must become perfect even as your Heavenly Father is perfect and let that which is imperfect go on its way. One day it will destroy itself.

"All must be reborn and dwell joyously on earth, for the Holy Earth was created in joy and love, and brought into being through the loving will of a loving father. To become one with earth is to rise beyond illness and pain, and to become one with heaven is to rise beyond hatred and war.

"Truly, those who do the will of your Heavenly Father are your true brothers and sisters, not your brothers and sisters by blood. Walk therefore in peace with your brothers and sisters, for united you possess a power greater than the mighty mountains and more eternal than even the sea. To walk as others walk, in unknowing and ignorance, is to embrace death and sorrow.

"I would have you know that those who seek the glory and wonder of peace must first learn to live in peace with all people, even those who are in poverty, those of different beliefs, those who are from a distant land and those whose skin is a different color.

"All who have been born on earth, whatever is their status, are children of God. He has brought all people into being and each is precious to him: those who are here, those who have gone, and those who live beyond the boundaries of the stars.

"You heart is like a great sea and can only be tempered by love and wisdom. As the waves become gentle under a windless sky, so does the heart of man rest when he has ceased to war against his fellow man.

"Only those whose hearts are stilled by the gentle breezes of understanding and compassion toward all living things will one day come face to face with God. Think you not that you shall see God, for He comes to all who strives to live in harmony with His Law."

One man spoke up, "Master, what you say is right, but it is difficult not to hate those who persecute us. Is there a way that we might remember your teachings and learn to live in harmony with the Law?"

When Jesus heard the man, he looked upon him kindly and replied. "It is well that you would ask for that which is righteous, for seven are the ways of peace. Remember these things I tell you and think upon them when the sun is high in the sky and all things are still, even the birds.

Pathway One – Peace with the Body:

As Jesus sat quietly it seemed that the whole of earth was silent too. Those who were with him did not speak, for it was not considered proper for followers or disciples to speak during discourses on the Law unless spoken to, or acknowledged.

Soon, however, Jesus began to speak again to those who were gathered around him, saying, "The first step toward peace is to find peace with your body, for when grievous pains consume your limbs your mind cannot think and you become filled with distemper. Do as I have bid you. Seek companionship with the sun, and the air and the water that you might live in good health.

Pathway Two – Peace with the Mind:

"The second Path is to seek peace with your mind, for all thoughts of malice place a burden upon your friends, your family and even others you must mingle with by day. Each thought of darkness destroys not only those who must receive it, but also upon the one who sends it.

"Know you, that the mind is like a great desert, wherein there is naught but sand and scorpions. Then the wind comes and scatters the sand because it has no roots. Neither has a mind any roots when hatred and anger consume it, for these are more powerful than even those winds that come to us from the distant hills. Thus, you must purify your mind and think only good thoughts. Then only good will follow after you.

"Seek therefore the wisdom that flows from the teachings of the Ancients, for a wise man tills the soil and plants the seeds of peace. Blessed are the wise of mind, for they shall create heaven on earth.

Pathway Three – Peace with the Family:
"The third path is to seek peace with those of your family. Be kind to those who are your parents, your children and your cousins, for they are a reflection of even a greater family. Know that we are of the same seed – the seed of our Heavenly Father. Know too, that the same mother nourishes us all, and she is this holy earth upon which we live.

"I tell you truly, it is oft times easier to love a stranger than those who dwell with us. Our brother and sisters, and even our mothers and fathers, have known our weaknesses and heard our words of anger. They have seen us naked and we are ashamed.

"Only love can heal the wounds caused by unbridled tongues and minds that run rampant. Only love is sweet like nectar to the bee, or rain upon the parched ground. Truly, one who does not love casts a dark shadow on all that he sees.

"The heart of he who is angry is like unto a restless sea and creates many enemies. But he who loves calms the war in his heart and becomes serene. A kind word is like honeycomb and turns your enemy into a friend, even as it brings peace to all your family."

Pathway Four – Peace with the World:

For a moment Jesus paused, as though to draw wisdom from some hidden power. Then he continued to speak to the people, saying, "The fourth path is a difficult path, for when you have brought peace to your own family then you must seek peace with all humanity.

"When the sun is high in the sky and the earth is silent, remember the whole of your earthly family and think upon the cities you have built and upon the grounds whereon you have all toiled. You have worked as one brotherhood since the beginning of time and you shall remain of one brotherhood forevermore.

"Although each must follow their path, each path is a part of the whole. Regardless of race or creed, everyone who lives has been created by the same hand, which created the stars. And blessed are those who build a peace upon the earth, for they shall commune in both in the world of men and the world of angels.

""Know this and remember it always: only those who create peace in the world shall have peace within themselves. Know you also, that there shall be no peace among peoples till there be one garden of the brotherhood over the earth."

Pathway Five – Peace with Culture:

"The fifth pathway of peace will be found in the knowledge of the ages that have heretofore passed before us. The ancients walked tall in might and thought, and they left their wisdom to lighten our path through the dark forest of misconception. Many are the Pharisees and Sadducees who would have you partake of their words, but they are as blind leading blind people.

"Only the ancient writings of the ancient wisdoms who once studied the law, can light a pathway through the dark forest of false ideas. Their words are based upon the Holy Law as it is expressed by God and revealed through nature.

"Know you that the written words of the wise will lead you to the unwritten words and teachings that nurture and guide all creation. Truly, the written Law is but a reflection of that which is unwritten.

"Wise are those who follow in the footsteps of the ancients and work for the brotherhood of all mankind.

Pathway Six – Peace with the Holy Earth:
"Then shall you seek peace with the earth. She is our Holy Mother and a living, breathing organism that sustains human existence. She provides all things for the health and healing of the body, rocks to sustain bones, water to purify, and fresh fruit for the well being of the body and herbs for healing.

"Those who eat not from the flesh of the earthly mother experience all manner of diseases. Their bones turn to dust, their body ages before it is time, and death claims the last remaining fragments of life.

"Long ago mankind turned away from the natural laws of earth and was drawn by sense attraction to those things that bring neither true happiness nor peace. Although such action was born through ignorance, the reprisal for this ignorance has been illness, old age and death.

"Because all mysteries are contained in the food that grows, the herb-yielding plants, the rivers and streams, and yea, even in our bodies, those who would possess great power must come into harmony with the ways of nature.

"Therefore pray thusly to your Earthly Mother, who hears your prayers even as your Heavenly Father hears your prayers, *"Our Father who art in heaven, send to all who walk upon the earth peace and joy, that we might live in harmony with our earthly mother, and in peace with our brothers and sisters."*

Pathway Seven – Peace with the Heavenly Father:
Sometimes as he talked, Jesus would look out over the Sea of Galilee, and yet other times he looked into the faces of the people

who had gathered to be with him. He not only held the minds of the people in his consciousness but he also lifted them. When Jesus began speaking again, he was of serious countenance, for his relationship with God was the secret of all his power. Therefore, when he spoke of God, he spoke with great reverence: to impress upon the people the importance of what he was about to say.

"Lastly, you must seek peace with God. It is He who has brought forth the sun, the moon, and the stars. Know you that you are in Him and He is in you, and that nothing can kill your soul and nothing can separate your soul from Him – except that you follow not His Law. Those who seek His kingdom shall know eternal life, for the soul knows no death.

"When each has reached that Light, which is brighter than the earthly sun, then shall they be taught by God's angels and come to dwell in His kingdom on earth and in heaven."

After this Jesus sat quietly and those who sat with him were silent also. The late afternoon light played hide-n-seek with the lapping waters as it set sail in the distant horizon. Soon the stars came out to play and the last shades of indigo and magenta faded into darkness as the moon rose in the sky.

As Jesus departed from them, the people did not speak, for they experienced a peace they had never known and they wished that it would not pass from them.

Section Two

FELLOWSHIP WITH THE ANGELS

Section Two

Introduction

The *Invocation of the Angels* are considered the second major section of the *Lost Jesus Scroll*. Body purification was, and still is, a prerequisite to the higher spiritual teachings. This is not to say that Jesus did not teach all who came to him. However, since the body is but an outer reflection of the indwelling soul, Jesus appeared to be partial to those disciples who first sought to purify the body.

As explained in Section I, the pathway to oneness with God is more difficult when the body is out of harmony with nature. At the same time, it is also important to remember that the body is only a physical manifestation of the whole, and therefore one should not believe that the body must be totally cleansed before participating in the Invocations. The mind actually enables mankind to reach for the stars, although it is the heart that unlocks the doorway leading to union with God. Neither of these can be wholly governed by the world of matter.

The Invocations are very subtle and it is easy to pass over them without putting them into practice. However, to do so would result in a great loss, not only because of the benefits that can be achieved through regular practice, but also in understanding the basic foundation of Jesus' miracles.

According to the *Lost Jesus Scroll*, Jesus taught his followers to abide by the daily ritual of morning, mid-day, and evening contemplation and prayer, perhaps because it would be virtually impossible for anyone to perform all fourteen of the primary Invocations on a daily basis. Therefore these were assigned to specific days of the week, not only to simplify their practice, but also to bring the consciousness into a deeper awareness of the progressive process of creation.

The *seventh day*, as previously mentioned, symbolizes the final epoch of creation when an enlightened mankind will bring heaven to earth. This was, and still is, looked upon as the Sabbath, or a holy day, and was honored because it signifies the final phase of the soul's journey through matter, or the end of the known world. In *St. John's Revelation* this day, or epoch, was represented by the descent of the *New Jerusalem*

Therefore, the primary meditations pertaining to morning and evening are presented here in the same sequential order as those outlined in the *Lost Jesus Scroll*, beginning with Saturday night at sunset.

SECTION TWO

CHAPTER 10

Jesus on Fellowship
with the Holy Forces of Natural and Cosmic Law

As the seasons passed, the intense heat gradually surrendered to the rains, and the rains eventually gave way to hail and snow. Again it was the month of Nisan, time of the spring equinox. The paschal lamb had been selected and preparations were being made to celebrate the Feast of the Passover. These festivities would last from the fifteenth day of Nisan, or Abib, to the twenty-first.

The Feast of the Passover, followed by the Feast of Unleavened Bread, was one of the great historical events sanctioned by Mosaic Law. As the lunar pastoral festival coincided with the lambing season, it fell on the fourteenth day of the civil year in conjunction with the spring equinox. The paschal lamb was killed on the evening of the fourteenth and heralded the beginning of the festival. People came from throughout the land to bring their offerings to the Temple. At this time, however, it was too dangerous for Jesus to appear in the city and he sought refuge in Bethany at the home of Lazarus and his sisters.

And it came to pass that some of the people learned that Jesus was in Bethany and they came to him. Among these was one young man who approached him, asking, "Oh good teacher, what is the best thing that I can do to achieve eternal life?"

When someone came to him in such a manner, Jesus would look upon him, or her, long and intensely. It was possible for him to see deeply into the heart of every soul, for nothing was hidden from him. In such a manner he could discern the future and the past, even as he could perceive a person's thoughts, weaknesses and strengths. Indeed, Jesus had chosen each of his disciples with the same discernment and insight.

Thus, after having looked at the youth before him for a brief moment with deep penetration, Jesus replied, "Do not call me good, for there is not one who is good except God. However, if you would find the key to eternal life, you must obey the commandments."

"And what commandments are these?" the youth questioned.

"They are the Laws of Moses," Jesus answered. "You shall not commit adultery, you shall not steal, and you shall not bear false testimony against another. After this honor your father, your mother, and your neighbor as yourself."

"But, Master," the youth replied, "I have obeyed all these from my boyhood, and still I walk in darkness. What other things must I do to break the barriers of death?"

Half studying and half analyzing the young man's countenance, Jesus became grave, for he knew that many were called to enter the narrow gateway to eternal life but few were chosen. Speaking kindly, he said, "If you wish to learn the mysteries of eternal life go and sell all your possessions and give the money to the poor. Then you will have a treasure in heaven. When you have done this, come and follow me."

With great sorrow the youth shook his head and walked away, for he had great possessions.

Turning to his disciples, Jesus said, "It is very difficult for a rich man to enter the Kingdom of Heaven, for his attachments to human life bind him to earthly things. I tell you truly it is easier for a rope to go through the eye of a needle."

When Jesus' disciples heard this they were astonished and one of them asked, "Who then can be saved?"

Gazing at his disciples intently, a familiar ripple of merriment danced across Jesus' heart, although he did not allow it to touch his lips. Soberly, he answered, "It is impossible for people to rise to such heights alone, but when God dwells with them, everything is possible."

And it came to pass that after the Passover, Jesus returned to the Sea of Galilee. Following their customary practice, he and some of his disciples departed from Jerusalem and traveled toward the Jordan River. This was a favorite time of the year for Jesus, as it was neither too cold nor too hot.

The wind was in the south and melting snows of Lebanon filled the Jordan, occasionally causing it to overflow the lower planes. The Barley harvest was beginning to ripen on the plains of Jericho and the uplands were brilliantly adorned with short-lived vegetation and colorful flowers.

Jesus knew that the hour of his departure from earth would occur during the next Passover and he still had much to teach his disciples. Thus it came to pass one day shortly thereafter that his disciples came upon Jesus sitting alone and looking off across the sea. They gathered near him, although remaining silent. They knew that he would speak when he felt it was time to do so.

Finally, Jesus turned and looked upon them with deep compassion and began to speak, "I tell you truly, as a son inherits his father's land, so have we inherited this Holy land from our Father. This land is not a land to be plowed and cultivated, but a sacred place within every soul. It is there that each must build the Holy Temple."

"And as a temple can only be raised stone by stone, so must each raise the true temple and home of God through the labor of their hearts and their minds.

"Know you not, that before the end shall come all people must raise this Holy Temple, and the Heavenly Father abide in them. This can be done through the ancient Invocations, for these unite the heart of man to the heart of God. Each must be lived, and thought, as well as spoken.

"All too often the mouth speaks words of worship, yet fails to either think them, or live them. So it is with the Scribes and Pharisees, who speak many words, yet their tongues reflect not only their minds, but also a dark abyss from whence no light has ever shown.

"The Invocations are like unto a bridge which spans two worlds, that of earth and that of heaven. Wise are those who seek to cross this bridge, for they shall become one with heaven. Only man can rise to such heights and commune with God, for it is not given to the animals or to the fish of the sea.

"The time has come for each of you to receive the gift of tongues. Only the holy Invocations will enable you to possess power and dominion over the forces of earth, and to cross that bridge into the heavenly kingdom. Then shall your world be filled with glory and the Heavenly Father will send forth his angels to watch over you and to teach you.

"And one day you shall enter into the oneness with the Heavenly Father, for this has been the destiny of man since the beginning.

"Hark to my words closely and receive the gift of tongues through the holy fellowship with earth and heaven.

"When you open your eyes in the morning and see the rising sun and your ears hear the birds singing sweetly, say to yourself, "This is a day that God has made, for He shines in the Sun and it is He whose voice flows through the birds.

"My soul is in Him and He is in me. Therefore, I will seek to walk this day in oneness with Him and in harmony with earth."

And one of the disciples spoke up, saying, "Albeit we have knowledge of the ways of earth, we cannot see the powers of the Heavenly Father. How then can we speak to that which is invisible to our eyes?

Suddenly, it was as though a great light shone around Jesus and for a moment he was silent. Then he began speaking once more, "You are but babes, who cannot yet see the wonder behind all that is visible. What you see before you is but a shadow of a vast heaven you cannot see. Know you, the earth and everything upon her is as a garment for that which cannot be seen.

"Long ago, before the worlds came into being, the Heavenly Father created all that was to come. Slowly, through the ages, that which was once only conceived was brought into existence. And when the earth had formed, God brought forth man, who was sent forth to build the Kingdom of Heaven on earth. Through earth, mankind learns the ways of earth, but through the Holy Invocations he will learn the ways of heaven and see that which cannot be seen.

"There is a deep mystery beyond the stars and this mystery became known to the wise ones of old. There are secrets buried in the moving river, and even greater ones hidden within the rays of the sun. If you could but understand the beginning of all life, you would also understand your end."

For a time, Jesus' disciples sat quietly and thought upon his words. They knew that these mysteries he was about to impart to them were not ones taught by the Scribes and Pharisee, nor were they given to the people, for the people were yet as children and could not understand them.

SATURDAY NIGHT
FIRST INVOCATION – POWER
(Creation of the Universe)

Before creation began there existed a singular and powerful intelligence. To many who perceived the systemic movement of the heavens, this consciousness became known as God. They perceived this intelligence was, and is, a creative force capable of manifesting and sustaining all life within a pre-established Divine Plan. However, this plan is difficult to define because of its simplicity, for in this simplicity exists a complex and expanding universe.

The Divine Plan of God is evidenced through everything that exists, but it remains an enigma for most because the plan contains a concept, or idea, as well as its ultimate completion. This Plan systematically creates a process of progression and must, of its nature, fulfill the purpose that is instilled in it. Therefore the universe continues its evolution and progression according to a predestined course. It spreads before the human senses in an everhanging panorama of beauty and pageantry, moving always toward its final destiny.

Because all things are in motion, all things are changing and all things are progressing. Thus every form of life is assured of continual advancement and ultimate equality

On the first evening after the Sabbath
Saturday night at sunset

As his disciples gathered around him, eager to hear his words, Jesus said, "The first of the Holy Invocations is that of Power, for it was the power of the Heavenly Father which created the universe. Therein is written the destiny of every living thing, including even the stars in the sky.

"I tell you truly, this same power expresses through all that you do. It is the power that tills your soil and yet brings forth your young, even as it moves the heavens.

"You believe the power which lifts your hands to the plow is naught but you. I say to you, that you have no power except that which is given by the Spirit of God and flows through you.

"If you do not believe my words, then who can say they know the reason for existence, or the day they will die? Nay, you do not know these things for such power is not yours, unless it has been revealed to you by the hand that created you.

"The power of the Heavenly Father moves through the universe, even as the fire flowed through the bush when God spoke to Moses. It moves the stars and causes the earth to turn in the heavens, even as it gives strength to the grain of wheat to grow toward the sun.

"If you but knew it, this power is many times greater in man than it is in the tiny seed. Yet each small seed forces its way through the darkness of earth in order to fulfill its purpose.

"Can you not see? There would be no life on earth without the power of God, for life is of the Spirit of God. It moves through you and through your young. It sets the water in motion that it might flow toward the Great Sea and bears witness of itself through the rays of the sun.

"Seat yourselves therefore with your face toward the heavens and close your eyes. With the eyes of your spirit see the beginning of creation when the universe was but beginning. Through the holy breath, draw into you that same power which built the stars."

Simon Peter spoke up and asked, "But Master, I know not how the universe looked in the beginning. Therefore, how am I to see it, even in my mind?"

"It is well that you asked," Jesus replied, "For as it is with you, so is it with the world. God's handiwork is all around us, but we see only with the eyes of our bodies, not with the eyes of our mind. Therefore, let your mind carry you to the point where you can see the spirit of God bring forth the stars. As you draw in your breath you shall feel the power of creation enter into your body. But as your breath travels outward, let your soul flow toward the stars.

"Some day, you will mingle with all creation as it was in the beginning and you shall become one with the power of your Heavenly Father.

"Then shall you remember this power of the Heavenly Father and allow it work through you, that your work might be made greater and your mind be filled with understanding you did not heretofore possess.

"Know you not, that the power of the Heavenly Father is there for all to use. It is He and His power, which moves through the body of man and heals the sick, even as He bequeaths wisdom unto the ignorant. It is also His power alone that makes it possible for man to commune with the holy angels and know those things yet to come.

"All who would seek oneness with God must perform their work upon the earth with thanksgiving, whatever be their station. Yet, the thoughts of each must also become those of kindness and love, even as the feelings of each must become those of non-malice, for these reflect the hidden power that moves through the whole universe."

Sunday Morning
Second Invocation – the Sun
(Giver of Life)

The first manifestation of visible light was thousands of suns. Science has referred to this as the period of the "Big Bang," or that great moment when a sudden explosion produced the beginning of the universe. Although this term is very descriptive and depicts the beginning of the known world as it is conceived by the human mind, the universe actually existed long before this in the form of a prototype. Therefore, each sun and planet also contains a prototype of its proper place in the universe, including our own sun

Because all of the planets within our own system are derived from our sun and sustained by it, the sun signifies the highest form of creative power visible to the human eye. To understand this is to understand the nature of our solar system and to understand our solar system is to understand the nature of the universe. Because every sun and every planet bears the perfect imprint of God's Divine plan it is possible to both understand and observe the continuity and ever changing immortal nature of the human race.

The first morning after the Sabbath
Sunday morning at sunrise

Early one morning, as Jesus and his disciples gathered by the Sea of Galilee, he spoke to his disciples, saying, "See the sun now high in the sky. It sustains life, heals and ripens the grains and fruit. It is the living power of a living God.

"To separate yourself from the sun is to embrace darkness, for the life force that flows through your bodies is lessened when you mingle not with the sun. Know you that your bodies are of sunlight even as they are also of the stars.

"In the beginning of time the heavens were filled with untold suns and they carried with them the power of the Heavenly Father.

"I tell you truly, you have a power within you that can unite with the sun for healing and regeneration. The sun has no mind by which to think, but you have a loving father who has endowed you with supremacy over plant and beast, and has given you the power of reason.

"Rise therefore early in the morning when the sun is rising also. Go then and sit before the sun and watch it as it spreads across the land, for in the beginning all creation came upon the earth after this manner.

"Watch how the darkness flees before the sunrise. For in the beginning, as the Heavenly Father brought forth the universe, the light of a thousand suns spread through the heavens. Then came forth life's beginning, first in the form of grass and trees, later as creatures of the earth and sea, and after this, man.

"It was the sun which brought forth the worlds and yet sustains them, even to this day.

"After you have seated yourselves, raise your face in greeting that you might pay homage for the bountiful gift of life has been made possible by the sun. After this, close your eyes and feel the sun's rays warm the whole of your body.

"As I have taught you, draw the sun's rays into the center of your body where the forces of heaven and earth mingle. And you will feel the heat and power of the sun enter your body and strengthen it. Truly, when the power of life flows through you, your strength and vitality will also increased.

"Go then into the world with renewed strength and till the vineyard of your Heavenly Father, that your labors of today produce a greater work than your labors of the past. And your life shall be long upon the earth and death shall hold no fear.

"Many are the ways of the sun and I would tell you more, but you must first learn these things. As you learn, more will be revealed to you. I tell you truly, the sun expresses the nature of God and reveals all that has ever been written or thought.

"Even so, the power of man is greater than the power of the sun."

Sunday Night
Third Invocation – Love
(Cohesive Force of the Universe)

Love is the common factor which unites the universe through the Law of Attraction. Love, however, as it is experienced through human emotion is but a shadow of the more perfect Divine love interpenetrating the whole of the universe. When God created the world of the stars, He created it out of his own substance. Therefore, that part of Him which is invisible remains the non-manifested, and it is this aspect of God that sustains everything visible to human eye, from the smallest blade of grass to the furthest star.

God's reason for bringing forth creation is simple. Nonetheless, simple things can quickly become complex when one tries to offers an explanation. God loves unconditionally. Because of this, He brought forth the suns, planets and earth and gave each form of creation - life. In such a manner they would grow and achieve the perfection that was instilled within the Divine Plan at the inception of the universe. God's reason for creation is simple and yet profound. He wants mankind to experience, at an individual level, the full magnitude of His plan and to share in it.

As each individual travels this journey they are destined to one-day rise victorious from the quagmire of human suffering. All that is human, or matter, is merely a shadow of true reality. Thus, mankind is part human and part divine and each will rise beyond humanness to express their God-like nature.

Because life has been brought forth within the Creator through Divine love, a unifying force exists throughout creation. Beyond the passion of the emotions, beyond even the mind, love prevails. For this reason it is natural for each to seek its own kind, as "like attracts like" expresses the unity that has always existed. In times of war, floods and famine, this may not always seem apparent. However, one has but to look at those who selflessly risk their live for others. This reveals the selfless self that exists beyond the shadows of matter and the true spirit of life unencumbered by the differences of country, race, or creed.

This love is expressed in human form through male and female, families and yes, even games, as loyalists inspire their favorite team by celebration and cheers. For those who know not the reason for their existence, love on earth seems temporal. In time, isolation, divorce and death separate all people. Earth is a great school and no one can give his or her soul into the hands of another for safekeeping. The soul is of God, and in time it must seek its true state of existence and its predestined immortality. When union has been accomplished between the soul and its immortal self, God, each individual has then completed the Great Work and becomes one with all life.

Love is the cohesive force and underlying principle within all things and the world cannot and will not end until the unity between all things has been established. In heaven there is no hatred, anger, or judgment. Therefore, Jesus taught an Invocation that would enable each human being to unite with the power of love and bring peace to earth. He instructed his disciples to invoke this wondrous force of love that they might purify their feelings.

On the second evening after the Sabbath
Sunday evening at sunset

One evening, as the sun was setting over the sea, and the sky was filled with the saffron and gold of sunset, Jesus said to his disciples, "There is no greater power than love. Love can overcome your enemy, tame the wild beast and make all who dwell on earth your friend."

"But Master," Thomas said, "It is hard to love those who hate us and persecute us. We have been taught that it is an eye for an eye and a tooth for a tooth. Now you say that we must love our enemies."

And Jesus replied, "True, it is difficult to love your enemy, but hate breeds hate and it must end somewhere. When the water is blocked it can go nowhere. When hate meets with love, neither doeth hate have any power.

"Tell me who is the more powerful? He who slays all in his path until there is naught left but dust, or he who shares in co-creation with God and builds a heavenly kingdom on earth?

"Even the wild beast can be tamed, but only through love. Love is the cohesive force of the universe and has brought all things into being.

"Hold out your loving hand to a beast, and because it was created also by the love of Heavenly Father it shall not harm you. The wildness of the animal is like unto the violent current of the river, which expends itself when its advancing force is blocked by the placid waters of a deep pool.

"He who does not love is filled with hatred and anger, and this hatred and anger destroys the body and the mind, even as it lays waste to the soul. I tell you truly, none shall enter the Kingdom of Heaven who does not love. Know you not, the world was created by the love of the Heavenly Father, and by that love He has given you unto yourselves in order to share in His kingdom."

"How then, Master," ask Thomas, "Can we build love when we hold evil in our hearts?"

Smiling at him, Jesus said, "Thomas, come sit with me here beneath the evening sky and raise your eyes toward the stars. See those stars high in the sky. They are like unto robe worn by the Heavenly Father, even as you wear clothes that cover your bodies.

"Think you that they share not life with us? They are a part of the Kingdom of Heaven, even as this earth is part of it.

"Those who love only their own families, or those who love only their friends love little, but those who love all upon earth and all within heaven are those who approach the throne of God.

"Close your eyes and think upon that love which flows into all things from the Heavenly Father. In the eye of you mind, see how God brought the heavens forth in the beginning. Draw that love which now is and will be forever more, and that same love that was at the beginning, into you through the holy breath.

"Allow the eyes of your spirit to take you into that pure love, which mingles throughout all of the stars. And you will feel oneness with the heart of Him who brought you into being."

After they had been silent for a time that each might commune with the nature of love in the silence of their heart, Jesus spoke again. "And when each evening you have thought upon the power of love which has brought all things into existence, on the morrow you shall go forth over the earth and spread the seeds of love. For only when all people love one another, will there be peace over the whole of earth, and only then shall the end come."

And Jesus' disciples knew he spoke great truths, and they sought the current of holy love, that they might awaken the hidden wealth within them that the world be made better because of them.

Monday Morning
Fourth Invocation – Water
(Sustainer of Life)

For centuries one of the greatest symbols of wisdom has been water. It can teach us much, as it represents unity and surrender in motion. As a single drop, water has little power, but unified it becomes sufficiently powerful to carve deep crevasses through mighty rock. Water is also an example of perseverance and patience. Without this precious liquid, life in its current form could not exist upon the earth.

When our planet first came into being, it was in part comprised of hot molten elements from the ethers and gasses from the sun. As this mass gradually moved into the cold exterior of space, water covered the surface of the earth and began to cool it. In time, these waters formed mighty oceans and rushing streams, which sustained the earth and brought forth life.

Like the sun, Water gives freely to all - the land, the plants and trees, the animals and to man. Because water gives of itself unconditionally, it has been referred to as a perfect expression of God. To better understand the reason why such homage has been paid to this wondrous substance which makes life possible on earth, one must contemplate its deeper nature.

Is it possible for a person to develop a better understanding of life through the study of water? The answer is yes, for water is an expression of both physical and spiritual unity. As previously mentioned, one drop of water has little power, but many drops become a powerful river. If similarly united, mankind would possess an even greater power and could overcome every obstacle of human existence.

Just as a river carves its way through great mountains as it moves toward the sea, mankind would also find a new world by turning toward the Great Sea, the Cosmic Consciousness of God. Anyone who did so, whether man or woman, would become more loving, giving, strong and wise, and become free of jealousy, anger, hatred, impatience and lack of perseverance. This would make possible the accomplishment of any goal and the surmounting of all odds, because the soul of mankind is eternal and the waters of earth are not. One day the waters will evaporate and become part of the mist and rain of new beginnings. But the soul of man will live forever.

Thus water is the perfect servant, as well as a pure reflection of God's nature, and for these reasons Jesus taught his disciples to commune with it. Through his Invocation of Water, every person has the potentiality to unite with this powerful force and increase their ability to love all life, even as they purify their feelings and emotions.

The second morning after the Sabbath
Monday morning at sunrise

And early one morning while the dew was still heavy on the trees, Jesus spoke to his disciples, saying, "Come, all of you, and gather with me at the river's edge and I will teach you the deep and mysterious ways of the water."

And Jesus' disciples rose and went with him to the river's edge, seating themselves beside him.

"See the river," Jesus pointed, "It gives to all. It nourishes the creatures of the water and feeds that which grows along its shore. It rises as vapor and falls again as newborn rain upon the fields, that it might supply the land and bring forth the food that we eat.

"I tell you truly, a single drop of water has little power of itself, but when it joins to the many drops it is so powerful that it can carve a path through solid stone.

"Listen to the parable of one whose troubles ran deep into the night, who groaned and lamented because his calamities and his troubles were many. Had he realized that his troubles were but rocks in the river of life he would have rejoiced, for then his eyes would be opened and he would see that he was being prepared for the kingdom of heaven, even as the water is made pure as it makes its way to the sea.

"Man has greater power than the river, or even the sea, if he but knew it. Yet he is blind to the ways of the Heavenly Father and to the ways of the Holy Earth. He sees only a tree where there is a tree and only a river where there is a river. He sees not the river as an essence of his own being, or that it reflects all which is eternal.

"You must become therefore like unto the river: give of your loving kindness to all you meet. This is the way of God. He turns not away from those who hold malice in their hearts, but rather He shows them the path that leads to Eternal Life.

"Turn your bodies toward the river and close your eyes. Draw in the rushing current and allow it to flow into your heart.

"Then feel the holy river flow throughout your body. Now you may direct it where you will because you are more powerful than the river.

"And you shall become one with the river and the sea. Its love shall increase your love for all things, even as your body and your feelings are purified."

The hours passed as Jesus' disciples sat by the river's edge. Soon they felt the power of the water. Then a deep thirst came upon them to drink from the river's fount, for they now hungered for its nectar.

Monday Night
Fifth Invocation – Wisdom
(Directive Power of the Universe)

The pathway to wisdom is often an intangible road, as it is often confused with the knowledge one gains from reading books and listening to verbal discourses. However, wisdom is not material and is primarily gained through the experiences of life.

Jesus speaks of this in Matthew, Chapter 13, as he discusses the Kingdom of Heaven with his disciple (Matthew 13:44-46):

> *Again, the Kingdom of Heaven is like unto treasure in a field: the which when a man has found, he hides, and for joy thereof goes and sells all that he has, and buys that field.*
>
> *"Again, the Kingdom of Heaven is like unto a merchant man, seeking goodly pearls:*
>
> *"Who, when he had found one pearl of great price, went and sold all that he had, and bought it.*

For thousands of years, the gift of wisdom has been referred to as the pearl of great price, or the philosopher's stone, and many great minds whose work has been passed down through the generations gave up all that they had for it.

To some, wisdom is considered the greatest of all powers, for it alone can rule over the senses and defeat ignorance. To please the self does not necessarily please the world. For example, while loud music may be appealing to one it can be disgusting those who must listen. However, the ones who have found the secret to wisdom understand that the works of God encapsulate the good of all people, places and things. Seeking to emulate Him, those no longer blinded by the enticements of the human world seek to work for the good of the whole.

In time, the great philosophers, scientists, and religionists discovered that only the good survives. All other things become a vague memory and are ultimately eclipsed by the greater works of those who have become known as the "Immortals." For this reason, those who would possess wisdom have always sought not only the work of the great wisdoms, but they also strive to emulate, or live, what they have learned.

Sometimes two lines from a great writing are alone sufficient to fully occupy a wise person throughout the day. For instance, the Master's words "love all people" are alone sufficient to possess someone, not only for a day but also for a lifetime. Thus the wise person will spend the entire day, or even weeks, in a sincere effort to love all existing life.

As the days pass, those who sincerely practice love will find that they possess a greater and greater utilization of this magical power. For no apparent reason every one seems to respond accordingly, thereby becoming kinder, more understanding and helpful. Had not the three little words, "I love you" been put into action, neither the wisdom behind these words, nor their innate power would have been discovered.

There is no greater wisdom than God's wisdom, or the Cosmic Consciousness of the creative principle. He created only one plan, and yet it governs everything seen and unseen. This plan has been established in such a fashion as to assure the equality, perfection and greatness of all living things. As mentioned earlier, the forward movement, or development of His plan, assures the constant evolution and progression of the universe.

Everything written whether it is in the form of music, or poetry, or expressed in the world of art, science, or religion actually reflects this divine wisdom. Therefore, those who unite with this power, whether they are educated or uneducated, have equal potential, in that God's wisdom is the underlining principle of all education and is directly available to all. For this reason, Jesus taught his disciples to invoke this mighty force of God that they might become wiser in all matters.

On the third evening after the Sabbath
Monday evening at sunset

And so it came to pass that one evening, again as the sun was just setting, Jesus came to be alone with his disciples.

At first they sat quietly. After a time, however, John asked of Jesus, "Master, your words contain more wisdom than those of the Scribes and Pharisees. Tell us how you are able to see and know things no other man has known?"

And Jesus replied, "Those who would come closer unto the Heavenly Father shall also have a greater understanding of all living things. At first we are like little children, who see something, but not the power that created it. We see the flower, but not the seed that gave it life, or the power in the seed that made the flower possible.

"Yet, one should not seek wisdom for the sake of wisdom alone, for then one becomes as a mind filled only with empty words that have no power.

"Wisdom is of God. In Him are the answers to all things. Therefore you must seek to become one with Him and all that you would know will be given unto you, even the secret of the stars."

Then one of the disciples spoke up, saying, "Master, we are not like you. We have no power save for that which moves our bodies. How can we come unto God, for we are not holy and divine?"

Maintaining a countenance of gentle peace, Jesus replied, "I say to you, that you are more holy and divine than you know, for even as I am of God and He is in me, so are you of God. The Heavenly Father created all things holy, both man and beast, but only man can perceive his own heritage and know that he is the son of a living God.

"Therefore, take no heed that you are not like unto me. First, seek ye the heavenly kingdom and all powers shall be yours. And one day you shall come to know those things you have not heretofore known.

"When you close your eyes, think upon the wonder of creation; the valleys, the trees and the great seas. Think of the sun and the moon. Is there any greater wonder than the light of the sun, which glorifies the sky by day, or the moon that governs the tides? I say to you that all these have been brought into being by the one wisdom that created all things.

"Think upon He who instilled power in a grain of wheat to become twenty grains, or the seed in woman which becomes a child playing in the sun. Think you not that any man is truly wise who has not come first unto the One who is all wisdom.

"Draw in deeply from the mind which has brought forth creation and even now continues to guide all the stars. Feel the mind of God flow through your mind. And when you have again opened your eyes, see things anew. I tell you truly; all living things today are but shadows of things yet to come.

"Allow wisdom to guide you in all that you do, lest you become like those who go down into a deep well and take all others with them. I say to you, ever since the beginning the blind have led the blind and the thousands follow them."

With these words Jesus finished speaking, and he slowly rose up and left his disciples that he might be alone to commune with God.

Tuesday Morning
Sixth Invocation – Air
(Life Force)

From the beginning, at least as the beginning is conceived today, all life everywhere has been in motion. This includes the suns and their planets, as well as animal and human. Galaxies move within an ever-expanding universe, caused by the forward motion of the Great Plan. Solar systems move in cosmic dance within the galaxies, and each planet rotates around its parent sun.

Although a body may be in limbo because a person is in sleep state, still the breath of life continues. Air is therefore a magic elixir. It sustains life and there is no existence without it.

In part, the air which mankind breathes is made possible by the motion of our planet, as well as the vegetation growing upon its surface. However, even the plants, while given credit for sustaining life on earth, appears to absorb this mysterious and magical, but invisible, substance. It processes some life force, which is then passed on for consumption by both human and beast.

Breathing brings many necessary and vital nutrients into the human organism, for air exists in and through the empty space surrounding every individual. This same space is filled with life from every star in the universe. Therefore the air, which makes human life possible, is filled with unseen forces and carried forth by the motion of the universe.

The utilization of this power flowing throughout the universe can be increased by one's ability to breathe properly. It is for this purpose that Jesus taught his disciples to use certain breathing techniques when performing the Invocations. For example, if one person tries to push another person over with only one finger it is unlikely they will have much success. However, if that same person consciously breathes in from all the forces surrounding them, and on the outgoing breath directs that same energy into the tip of the finger through mental control, they will then be able to push a strong man over quite easily with one finger. Thus, air is not only life giving, but also very powerful.

The third morning after the Sabbath
Tuesday morning at sunrise

While Jesus sat with his disciples one morning as the sun was rising, he taught them about the power of the air, saying, "Feel the breath you draw in. Although you know it not, it contains forces gathered from the far away stars.

"In the beginning the Heavenly Father gathered a life force from non-manifested space to bring forth creation. Thus between the breathing in and breathing out are hidden all of the mysteries of life.

"I tell you truly that even when a suckling babe breathes, it draws power from the plants and heavens, causing its body to stretch until it one day it becomes an adult. Even so, no one knows the power that made this wonder happen.

"Truly the power of breath is to be honored, for a breath drawn from earth feeds your body and a breath drawn from heaven feeds your soul.

"Thus breathe in slowly and deeply, that you might feel this power enter your body. Know that it brings with it the essence of all the waters flowing over earth and the green grass waving in the wind. Feel it flow through your body as it would flow through a tree and feel it as it strengthens and regenerates every part of you.

"Lift your eyes to heaven and as you breathe in the breath of God you will feel that same power that has been since the beginning.

"As your breath flows outward, travel in the eye of your mind to the central core of God's holy breath. There you shall become one with Him, even as you were one in the beginning."

And all things were still as Jesus and his disciples sat quietly in the morning sun. With each incoming and outgoing breath they moved closer the Heavenly Father.

Tuesday Evening
Seventh Invocation – Eternal Life
(Immortality of the Soul)

Proof of immortality exists in everything on earth. However, immortality does not mean that the outer, or physical, expression of life remains as it is. Religious, philosophical and scientific evidence proves that the world is in a constant state of flux, or change. This applies not only to those things created by human hands, but all creation. Change is apparent everywhere and at all times, from the continued outward expansion of the universe to human appearance.

Scientific research and anthropological evidence point to the systematic progression of earth, for the Africanus Australopithecus of five and a half million years ago is now the Homo sapien of the modern world. In the world of tomorrow, the Homo sapien will likewise evolve into a new and more advanced being. This does not mean that life, as we know it, will cease; but rather it will gradually change.

All too often the world is evaluated according to its visual image and not its deeper reality. While death is actually a beautiful and wondrous outcome of having been born, many living in the world of matter feel only sorrow and loss when death occurs. These feelings are experienced because most people fail to look beyond the physical expression to the soul, and it is the soul that is immortal. It is also the soul, which moves into and occupies a body for a short span upon the winds of time in order to experience all things. From these experiences it eventually advances to the next level of progression, and when a body wears out much like a suit of clothes, the soul moves on - but where?

What planet among the millions of galaxies can be called heaven and what planet can be called hell? In reality, when the gross body is shed there still remains the semi-light, semi-material and true body of the soul. Thus the soul continues at a higher vibration than that of earth. Such a vibratory frequency is no longer invisible to the human eye.

In the *Lost Jesus Scroll* Jesus does not speak of death as the cessation of existence, but rather as a link with all life everywhere. If, there is a God, and the universe is contained within Him, then there can be no cessation of life, for cessation of life would be cessation of God. The Apostle Paul speaks openly about this in Corinthians 3:16, "Know ye not that ye are the temple of God and that the spirit of God dwells in you?"

Moses also mentions this when he refers to the seventh day, or seventh epoch, of earth's creation in Genesis II: 2, when he said:

> *And-he-fulfilled, He-the-God in the light's manifestation-the-seventh, the sovereign-work which he had-performed; and-he-restored-himself, in-the-light's manifestation-the-seventh, from-the-whole-sovereign-work which-he-had-performed. (Translated: from original Hebrew.)*

These words indicate that during the final dispensation of earth's passage through matter, God will come forth in all mankind. Thus death can be nothing more than the cessation of human life, while immortality is the reality underlying all physical manifestation.

On the fourth evening after the Sabbath
Tuesday evening at sunset

The day was hushed and still as Jesus sat with his disciples in the Garden of Gethsemane beneath the olive trees. The Master came here sometimes to be alone, and at other times to be with his disciples, for there were some of them who could not always travel with him.

As it was late in the day, the setting sun caused the dull green leaves on the branches of the olive trees to be deeply outlined against the encroaching night. It was during this panorama of day's surrender to night that Jesus sat down beneath one of the larger trees and began speaking to his disciples.

"See how the sun sets, yet it will rise again and again in its time. Life is like the olive leaf, it is a shadow and naught else but a reflection of that which is eternal.

"Know you that the son of man is more than he seems. Yet it is only with the eyes of the spirit one can experience the tie that binds everyone to life everywhere."

At this time one of the disciples spoke up and asked, "What do you mean, the eyes of Spirit, for I know only these eyes that now look upon you."

And for a moment a slight touch of amusement shone in Jesus eyes, for his disciples were also like his children, to be raised and reared. Finally he replied, "Your eyes that look upon me now see but a shadow, for they see only that which is visible. As you have eyes in your body so have you the eyes of spirit. When you see with the eyes of your spirit you will see a beauty greater than earth and then you will meet the angels face to face.

"Close therefore your eyes and do not look upon death and decay. Instead, look with the eye of your mind into the vast empty space beyond the boundaries of this world. Then darkness will fade away and you shall see light.

"Know you that this light is the doorway to your true home.

By day our feet must walk the earth, but with the coming of the night we overcome our bondage to earth and join that which is eternal.

"Do you not feel yourself when your eyes are closed? I tell you truly that this self you feel is within the body, but not of it. This is the spiritual body of which I have spoken and it is your eternal self. Your eternal self cannot be injured, nor does it die. Yet, it matures and changes, becoming more and more like unto an angel, until one day it hath no more need of its human confines. When this has come to pass you shall then leave behind the bonds of earth and dwell in the heavenly kingdom forever.

"Know that this self is one with all living things. Experience that unity you do not feel when you are drawn to the outside world by your bodily senses, and experience the inner peace that comes only when the soul has withdrawn from the outer world. Know you not, this is the true nature of man and you were thus even before the world came into being.

"Do not believe that the death of the body will reveal this great mystery. If you know not God while you live upon earth, and know not that He created you immortal, you will continue to walk in naught but shadows in the days that are yet to come.

"Open wide the eyes of your spirit and dwell not in flesh while upon the earth, but rather in your true body. Then you shall walk among the angels, even as you walk among men. And you shall live in both worlds, knowing that the time will come when you must depart from the flesh, but it shall be without fear or sorrow.

Wednesday Morning
Eighth Invocation – Earth
(The Holy Mother)

Rains, similar to those now falling on Venus, gradually cooled the molten mass of gasses and ether called earth. As the earth cooled, a crust formed and life began. This contained all of the organic material necessary to create and sustain life. The crust was filled with minerals from the fiery inferno of molten lava spewing from great volcanoes, and the rain eventually became running rivers and great seas. These rivers and seas moistened the earth and cooled the lava, and in time the earth produced foliage.

The earth has never been an inert mound of matter floating through chaotic space. Given that it systematically rotates around it parent sun it takes its proper place in the universe. Thus, it is a holy and breathing organism, whose existence was formulated as part of the Great Plan in the beginning of the universe.

For centuries, many believed that earth was the center of the universe and that the suns and stars moved around it. However, because of the revolutionary work of Copernicus and Galileo, the astronomers of antiquity had to take another look at the movement of heavenly bodies. At the time, of course, the work of Copernicus and Galileo was branded as *heretic* by the church because their theories took away the supernormal significance of Earth and cast it as just one planet in the systematic movement of the stars.

Even more regrettable, some people, even today, believe that earth - one planet in millions of galaxies - was actually literally built in seven days. To view it differently would once again take away the supernormal attributes of earth for those who believe in the wondrous miracle; that this earth alone has God's divine blessing. Nonetheless, others still look upon earth as a piece of inert matter and not a living and breathing or organism. Because of such beliefs the earth suffers great pollution, and in some countries terrible unsanitary conditions bringing death, deformity and multiple diseases. If mankind truly understood earth, then it would also possess the wisdom to know that to destroy the earth is to destroy the human race.

Jesus certainly looked upon earth as both a living and holy organism and he referred to it in the *Lost Jesus Scroll* as the Holy Mother. The Master taught his disciples to pay homage to the earth's topsoil, because it was the producer of life. He knew that the soil contained all of the necessary nutrients to enable a single grain of wheat to become twenty, or an acorn to become a tree.

The fourth morning after the Sabbath
Wednesday morning at sunrise

As Jesus taught his disciples concerning the life force existing within the soil, he said, "I say to you, look with your eyes toward the horizon where the earth and the sky mingle, and then beyond the distant hills and even beyond the sea. Know you not that you walk upon holy soil and that wherever you place your feet is a living expression of a living God?

"You should know this, for daily you partake of the soil's bountiful harvest and receive life in return. Yet you would lay waste to the earth, which is as a mother to all living things. You care not that she becomes starved and filled with disease, because you know not that her death is your death.

He who tills the soil and plants seed into the ground is truly a husbandman to the earth and she shall reward him richly with rich grains and ripened fruit.

"Truly, you do not understand the power of life that flows from this holy plant into the body of man, for you do not see it.

"Come and I will teach you, that you might understand the holy nature of earth and partake of the wealth she contains."

"Close therefore your eyes that you might turn away from those things of the outer world and feel the power that flows through all creation."

And when those who had gathered with Jesus closed their eyes and became silent, Jesus said to them, "Feel the earth and the living force beneath you that intermingles with the soil. If you would but know it, this force gives you life, even as it also heals.

"To better understand these things I say, seek to draw this fire upward through your body and you will feel its flame fill you with life. It is like unto the rays of the sun and the flow of the river, and its power will regenerate your body.

"Open wide the eyes of your mind, and mingle with the grain growing on the hills and the fruit trees giving of their fruit. And you will feel the holy breath of your holy mother, who will tend you and care for you if you will but obey her laws.

"I say to you that the power of your Mother Earth is many times greater than that of your mother by blood, and her love knows no end, nor has it any boundaries."

And when he had ceased speaking there was silence. It was as though the earth stood still and all living things paid homage to the Holy Mother who gave them life.

WEDNESDAY EVENING
NINTH INVOCATION – CREATIVE WORK
(Highway to Heaven)

It is a misnomer to conceive that God rested upon the seventh day of the week, if for no other reason than the irrevocable fact that life never ceases in its movement. Although not readily visible to the human eye, the stars are in constant motion both day and night. The earth continues to rotate around the sun in a systematic pattern, along with all of its neighboring brother and sister planets. Spring, summer, fall and winter all burst forth in great splendor, without ever halting in their systematic renewals. Everywhere, every hour of the day and year, the creative work of an ever-expanding universe continues.

Why then the Sabbath? Most of the ancient ones who reached union with God were privileged to view His Divine Plan. Therefore they knew that human life would one day cease to exist in its present state. However, they also knew that this would not occur until every human being had united with the Light of God within them. In turn, this would transform them from human during what the ancients refer too as the Seventh Epoch, or seventh day of creation.

Because God and man are pre-destined to become one, the seventh epoch has always represented the holy period when peace will come to earth. This state can only be achieved through the creative work of each individual, for it is only by the raising of the consciousness of God within that mankind can reach his true greatness. Therefore, this seventh epoch will be approached individually as well as collectively.

To symbolize the fulfillment of this final stage of progression yet to come upon earth, the ancient ones established a holy day and referred to it as the Sabbath, a symbolic representation of the final phase of earthly progression. Therefore, on the seventh day of the week people were, and still are, asked to pay homage to God, by living that day as it will be lived when the final journey through matter is completed.

On the eleventh hour, signifying the beginning of the union between the soul and its divine counterpart, the personal life is left behind to join in an hour of worship. At twelve O'clock the two natures become one (1-2), a period both preceded and followed by withdrawal from the corporeal world and cessation to earthly attachments.

To strengthen his disciples' understanding in the necessity of creative work, Jesus sought to express the concept that all things move and progress only through individual effort. (As one grain of wheat becomes twenty grains.)

On the fifth evening after the Sabbath
Wednesday evening at sunset

Departing from the house of Lazarus with some of his disciples Jesus returned to Capernaum along the silent desert shores of the Jordan River. After walking some distance the group made a sharp left turn, following the old boundary line separating the tribe of Judah from the tribe of Benjamin.

The long descent was bounded on the south side by the wild gorge of the Kelt. Across the barren plains rested the sparkling Dead Sea. Its water was perfectly clear and transparent, but its taste was bitter and saltier than even the ocean. For those who dared to sample it, the Dead Sea's water acted upon the tongue and mouth like alum, and irritated the eyes like camphor. This produced a burning, prickling sensation.

The atmosphere was like a vast funeral pall dropped from heaven, and it hung heavily over the lifeless bosom of the mysterious lake before expanding over the entire area below Jericho.

As the small group descended into the desert, the profound gorge of Wady Kelt lay beneath them, and on the north, the ridge of Quarnantana with its caverns, cells, and rock-hewn chapels. The impenetrable silence of the land seemed to forbid speaking and so the small group made its way quietly without conversation.

The Master was also silent. Here in the desert he was free from the raucous vibrations of the cities and a deep peace penetrated his soul. Jesus drank heavily of the isolation for his nomadic years had made him akin to the intense heat, the shifting sands and moving winds of the desert. In no other place did he feel so free and yet so much one with the powerful forces of nature and the universe.

On arriving in Jericho, Jesus and his disciples reached the high plateau, known as the Ell es-sultan. There the Master paused for a moment to view the panorama of the valley below him. This remarkable city rested between the wide plain where the Jordan Valley broadened between the Moab and Edom precipices. From here Jesus could see the vast plains and sandy mountains, crowned with the ancient memories of some of the grandest events in history.

After a brief pause to look upon the wonders of nature the group began to walk again. When they arrived in Jericho, Jesus and his disciples went into the center of the city to seek food and lodging, satisfied with a frugal fare and palate of straw under the stars. However, by the time night fell, word had gone out through Jericho that Jesus had come, and people came to him that they might be healed.

And it came to pass that Jesus stayed and taught the people of Jericho for several days, after which he took his disciples and departed once more for Capernaum.

Later the master spoke to those who were with him, saying, "Know you, that deep within you is the cause and purpose of your existence. He who has found his cause in life need not ask for any other blessing.

"But how shall we know our task?" one asked.

"You will know your task only through effort. First you must seek the Kingdom of God. Then all will be given to you. Until then you must work in the field of the world that you be found worthy to follow the purpose for which you have been created.

"Those who work not in the vineyards of the Heavenly Father shall forever be in want, not only by hunger in their body, but by idleness, which causes them to do many evil things. Their nights are filled with bitterness and hatred. In envy of those who have more than they, they plot to plunder and lay waste to their enemy's garner.

"A mind that is idle allows seeds of discontent to take root and destroy all that is good. Know that those who work in the Garden of the Brotherhood, whether it is the planting of the fields, or the making of shoes, are dear to the Heavenly Father. He rewards them openly by filling their tables with an abundance of fresh fruit and golden grain.

"Truly, all things that live upon earth must perform creative work. The flowers give freely of themselves to the bees that the bees might prepare honey; even as a shepherd must remain wakeful, less his flock goes astray. The sun gives life to all living things and the water nourishes all who come to drink from its wells and streams.

"Only through creative work can heaven and earth become one. Yet, your work must be as the work of all creation. You must serve all the children of your Heavenly Father by giving to the poor, even as you may take payment from the rich. The Heavenly

Father knows all your needs, and as your serve him, so shall He supply your needs in many unknown ways.

"You have heard it said that you shall worship on the Sabbath day and keep it holy. I say unto you that every day is holy, for the Lord works without ceasing in order that the world may continue to grow and live.

"Think you not that you can walk in the ways of God and yet live in idleness. He who is idle is like unto the grape that has not yet brought forth its wine.

"No man shall come before the Heavenly Father who has not fulfilled his purpose on earth, nor shall any man open the door to the Kingdom of Heaven who has not labored upon the earth. Until every person works for the good of all others, there shall be no peace upon the earth, nor shall earth pass away.

"Close your eyes therefore, that you might think upon creation as it was in the beginning. See you not, that the creation continues throughout both the day and the night. Therefore, the work of your Heavenly Father also continues without rest, for it is He who plants the stars in the sky and brings forth the abundance of earth. Feel this power flow through the whole of your body.

"Then allow your mind to flow outward and mingle with creation as it was when the universe began. Think upon the wonders of Creative Work, for it brought forth and sustains the stars on their rounds, and it makes the tree to grow, and the flowers produce their bloom."

For a time Jesus and his disciples sat quietly with closed eyes so that they might co-mingle with the power of creation. New life began to flow within them and they remembered those times they had worked side-by-side in the fields and gathered fish from the sea.

After some time had passed in silence, Jesus spoke again, saying, "God comes forth in the glory of dawn to awake you from your sleep. Therefore, obey his command and do not lie idle in your beds, for the miracle of life awaits you without.

"Work in the vineyards of the world all the day with a happy heart and allow the power of love to flow from you heart. It is then that you will come to understand these things I teach you."

And the people were touched by the words Jesus spoke, for each sought peace. Daily they prayed that Israel would become as it once was following the days of Moses. And as they looked one to another, each knew that they must go forth and bear fruit in order for the world to be made better.

Thursday Morning
Tenth Invocation – Life
(God's Visual Expression)

When the earth's surface finally cooled, all of the nutrients necessary for life were present in the grasses, rivers and trees. Creeping, crawling, swimming, and upright creatures evolved from their primitive beginning and began to dwell upon land. In time, human life appeared and they became co-creators, for they went forth and discovered methods to tame the earth's surface and preserve their life.

Because the reason for existence was mysterious and could not be understood, the people paid homage not only for their own life, but also for all of the things that preserved it. In the pagan rituals this went so far as to offer sacrifices of humans, and later, animals. It was believed that such honor would help preserve life and offer protection from volcanoes, drought, and pestilence

The mysterious and invisible substance that flowed through the body, causing it to walk and talk, was looked upon as holy. It was believed that a Holy Spirit activated all life, and that this same Holy Spirit was an essence descending directly from the Creator who had brought the universe into being. And in a way this belief is true. Life was brought forth through the Creative Work of the Heavenly Father and is reflected in the rising sun, the budding flowers, and other life forms everywhere.

Each dawn reenacts the wonderful phenomena of creation, as its light slowly rises above the horizon and gradually illumines all that darkness has hidden. At sunrise, life begins to stir, as though activated by some unseen power. At the same time the unrevealed is now revealed, as it was when the world began.

In the Lost Jesus Scroll Jesus tries to help his disciples understand this invisible nature of life. He does this by pointing out the living expressions of nature, which existed everywhere, particularly grass the oldest living thing on earth.

The fifth morning after the Sabbath
Thursday morning at sunrise

Jesus sought to explain life to his disciples one morning as the sun sent forth its rays upon the tender green plants. On this particular day, the master chose to meet his close followers underneath one of ancient trees along the river's edge. They approached him quietly, for he appeared to be concentrating deeply on a small vessel he held in his hands. However, as they came near Jesus looked upon them kindly and motioned for them to be seated near him.

"It is good that you have chosen the path of righteousness," the Master said to them, "for you have entered unto the path of immortality and now walk in the path of truth, even as the great ones did before you. You are learning to see and hear with the eyes and ears of spirit, where the air flies high against the azure sky, where the sun reigns supreme above the clouds and where the glistening water flows in the streams of life.

"The time has come when I can speak to you of deep and mysterious things, for the grass which grows in this earthen pot I am holding in my hands is more powerful than the mighty thunder. It hides its grandeur after the manner of a great ruler of old, who once disguised himself as a beggar and visited the village of his subjects. He knew that the people would open their hearts to a simple man, but if they knew who walked among them, they would fall at his feet in fear.

"I tell you truly, that the blade of grass carries a force of life that sustains all living things, even as it endures the ravages of the wind and fire. It was brought forth with the seas and the mountains and has lived since the beginning of earth"

Then one of the disciples who sat near him looked upon the earthen pot that Jesus held and saw that it contained only wheat grass like that which grew in the lower valleys, and he asked, "How is the grass that you hold in your hand different than that growing on the hill?"

"It is not different," Jesus replied. "Every growing thing is a part of earth. Yet when we separate these blades of wheat from the fields, it is possible to also touch the very force of life, which brought forth creation.

"It is not unlike this sacred tree now protecting us with its branches, for there is much power in this tree. It is like unto a brother to us, giving shade and shelter to all who come into its care.

"If you would but know it, this mighty tree draws the force of life up through its roots and sends it throughout all of its branches. It will give also to us, if we will but come unto it in Holy Invocation.

"Close therefore your eyes, and in the eye of your mind embrace your brother tree as you would embrace your brother by blood. Draw deeply from the force of life that flows through it. Allow the forces of life from your brother tree to enter into all parts of your body. And with the eyes of your spirit direct it to that place within you that has need for healing and life.

"Feel the tree's strength become your strength, for if you but knew it our Brother Tree bears the power of God in its trunk and in its branches."

When Jesus finished speaking he sat quietly, and as he closed his eyes waves of light radiated around him, shimmering as brightly as the sun. He continued to sit silently, even as the shadows of the day lengthened. Soon every living thing around ceased paying him heed, for it was as if he had disappeared into a world where no one could follow.

Thursday Night
Eleventh Invocation – Peace
(Living in Harmony)

The cry for peace has risen throughout the ages. It reverberates in every soul, even as a cry goes out for one nation to bear arms against another. Often concern for peace is centered only in the cessation of war, but there can be no real lasting peace until there is peace within every heart. To cease war would be very easy. Everyone, everywhere, would simply have to lay down his or her battle arms and refuse to fight. Yet, as a people, we do not seem ready to participate in such a simple thing.

Great spiritual leaders throughout the centuries have tried to instill the pathway of peace into generations of humanity, for peace must be established in the individual before it can reign supreme over earth. For this reason, the focus is now on the development of individual inner peace. Yet, how can there be true inner peace when hate, anger and jealousy still have their seat in the heart?

Peace must, of its very nature, become dual action. One must work toward inner peace in order to have outer peace and one must work toward outer peace in order to have inner peace. For this reason Jesus taught both aspects. Not only did he teach his disciples to overcome the harmful emotions ruling over their minds and their bodies, but also to go forth among the people and live in peace among their fellow man.

To live peacefully is more difficult than it may seem, because the world as a whole still follows a path of destruction. It will not always be this way, of course, for a peaceful co-existence must be manifested in the world before the human race can move on. This is the task that has been assigned to mankind since the beginning, even before the universe was formed.

The lack of spiritual education, not religious education, is one of the primary reasons why civilization moves so slowly toward its destiny. Many people do not understand the nature of the universe, the systematic progression of all life, and that a perfect law of cause and effect prevails. No action, nor thought, escapes God's Divine Law. Although the Courts may acquit a guilty man, there is a supreme spiritual justice that sees that all unlearned lessons are eventually learned. If each individual understood that they must one day account for every deed and thought before passing from human into divine, perhaps they would take greater care to preserve life. Sometimes it seems that the weapons of war are far easier to develop than the weapons of peace, such as love, compassion and understanding.

It is for the purpose of peace that Jesus taught not only his seven-fold path of peace, to be practiced when the sun was high in the sky, but he also taught his disciples that heaven and earth could not unite until peace was created on earth.

On the sixth evening after the Sabbath
Thursday evening at sunset

And it came to pass; as the northeasterly winds blew across the bleak hills now dry from months without rain, the land was in great turmoil. It was not a good time for political offenders, or for those who took a stand against the gradual encroachment of the political power of the Romans. However, this did not stop Jesus from teaching. If anything, he increased his efforts to prepare his disciples for the day when he must leave them.

"Happy are those who persevere to the end," Jesus told his disciples, "for any violation of the Law of the Heavenly Father and those of earth are written in your souls and you must bear the pain thereof.

"No one makes an error, but that it is not written within them. One may escape the laws made by man and kings, but none can escape the Law of God. And when you have raised the dead (the indwelling divine nature) you will come before the face of God, and all that is written in your souls shall bear witness of you, both good and evil.

"After this you must make right those things written in the book of your soul, through good thoughts, good deeds and good words. Then you shall be forgiven. And the Heavenly Father will prepare a place for you in the Kingdom of Heaven and make you ruler over many things on earth.

"Many and grievous are the sufferings of the people when they do not give love to all others, for he who is without love casts a dark shadow on everyone he meets, most of all upon those with whom he lives. His harsh and angry words fall on his brothers like fetid air from a stagnant pool. I tell you truly, he who speaks words of darkness suffers most, for the darkness that encloses him is as the dank smell of a musty tomb.

"If one has no love, they build a wall between themselves and all the creatures of earth, and therein must dwell in loneliness and pain. And each becomes as an angry whirlpool that draws all that is too near into its depths. Peace must be built within and without before the world can be at peace

"Let us sit here by the lake's edge that we might feel the peace abiding in the quiet of the night and silent moving stars.

"Look above you. See, the moon is full. It knows not anger, nor hatred, but casts its light over the whole land. It does not give peace of itself, yet it reflects peace, for it mingles with the silence of the evening.

"Listen to the silence of the night. Do you not hear the sound of peace where the water touches the land, and in the darkness now resting upon the distant hills? I tell you truly, there is a sound within the silence and soon I shall teach you to hear beyond hearing and see beyond seeing."

Although Jesus' disciples puzzled over his words, they knew that they should not ask what he meant. Because they had traveled with him they knew that there was a time to ask and a time to remain silent. This was a time to embrace the silence.

After a pause in order for those who were with him to bear witness to the silence, Jesus spoke again, "Seek peace in all that you do and in every word you speak, for where peace dwells naught there is but a dark pit from whence there is no way to escape.

"Turn your face toward the light that flows from the moon and close your eyes. Feel the stillness of the night embrace you. If you but knew it, this stillness is like unto the embrace of your Heavenly Father, for He is all around you. Yet, you feel Him not when you walk in the hours of the day, for your eyes see only the world that is without.

"When you no longer see the world, feel only the sweet breath of peace as sleep enfolds the land and the hands of war are silenced. Draw this peace into your body, and into your mind, and your soul, and you will feel its healing power bring calm to your mind and ease the pain in your soul.

"Allow yourself to bathe in the holy stream of peace. There you will feel the presence of God and you will be surrounded by the light of the Kingdom of Heaven."

As Jesus' disciples sat with him within the silence of the full moon's radiant light, they knew that this peace they felt was the presence of God abiding with them. And they knew that as it was with them, so would it one day become the way of the world.

FRIDAY MORNING
TWELFTH INVOCATION – JOY
(Gateway to Happiness)

Although everyone wishes for happiness, it can never be achieved on a permanent basis until there is peace. Therefore, as the world moves toward its seventh epoch of planetary progression the earth is faced with finding ways to bring peace, not just a quietus between nations, but harmony between people. Only then will the happiness instilled in the Divine Plan become an integral and constant part of human existence.

For this reason the Invocation of Peace preceded the Invocation of Joy, for there can be no lasting joy until mankind has brought the world to peace. To many, it may appear that such an achievement is impossible, given the strife between nations, individual beliefs and customs, and races. However, that is what the seventh epoch is all about. It is a period of purgation, which will remove the residual of human dissension and ultimately prepare the entire human race for a greater field of endeavor.

In the meantime, joy is not dead. Joy is all around us, but we must cease the mad pace of worldly existence from time-to-time in order to find it. As there are periods of happiness in the lives of every human, the fallout from this happiness gathers itself like a giant river and becomes available to those who seek a moment of respite from worldly cares. To be happy means that one must work at not only being happy within them, but they must also touch others with it. It is a rule that those who give also receive, be it happiness, or kindness.

One source of happiness is to turn toward the beauty of the natural world, such as the snow-covered mountains, the moving clouds and the dancing flowers. In that these are only visible during the daylight hours, Jesus taught that the Invocation of Joy should be practiced at sunrise. This would in turn help to establish greater harmony within the soul and the mind throughout the day.

The sixth morning after the Sabbath
Friday morning at sunrise

As the disciples journeyed with Jesus, he joined them in the early morning and then sat with them again in the evening, continuing to teach them things in secret that could not be taught to the multitudes. When they practiced the disciplines of his teachings, the disciples found that a greater unity existed between themselves and those forces surrounding them. This transformation set them apart from others, for they became kinder and more at peace with all whom they met.

Even as the first faint glimmer of spiritual rebirth fell upon the disciples, their bodies began to regenerate much more easily. They seldom knew illness. Wild animals were stilled in their presence, and the poisonous creatures of the desert virtually ignored them. Yet other things occurred also, for the Invocations at sunrise brought the disciples a strength and oneness with God few people have ever experienced, and a strange new wisdom began to penetrate their unbridled minds.

During this awakening, the Master observed his disciples with the pleasure of a father, the kindness of a brother, and the power of a teacher. Yet, Jesus' followers did not know this, for his pleasure over their progress was hidden beneath the controlled outer mask of one who knew there was yet much for them to learn.

Early one morning when the sky was bathed in the multicolors of a newly awakened day, Jesus spoke to those who were with him about joy. He said, "This earth was brought into being through the love and joy of a loving God. He is not to be worshipped with sadness and cries of despair, but in love and gratitude for the life he has given you.

"Can you not rejoice that you have been given life? Like those who followed Moses in the Wilderness, you moan with despair when all around you is not as you would have it.

"I tell you truly, man was given dominion over the plants and the animals, but it was not given to him to rule over the earth or the stars. There is but one who possesses such power and that is He whose hands have shaped all that we see and who has breathed life into our souls and into our bodies.

"Can you not then rejoice, even though an ill has fallen upon you? Know you not that all ills are but lessons yet unlearned and perfection yet unwrought. Do not moan and bewail your lot, but go forth in the fields after the rains and smell the sweet odor of the blossoms. I say to you, a flower has no other purpose than to bring joy to those who dwell upon the earth.

"Listen with new ears to the sound of the birds as they sing their melody in the sunrise. Truly, there is no greater beauty than the colors that touch the morning sky at dawn or the sweet song of the birds.

"All these things have been given to you to make joyful your life and no one comes before Heavenly Father whom beauty and joy has not touched their hearts.

"Sit here with me and close your eyes that you might see with greater eyes and hear with greater ears. Think upon the flowers that dance when they are touched by soft winds of summer.

"Smell not only the sweet fragrance of the flowers, but also bask in their joy as they open their blossoms toward the heavens. And their joy shall become your joy.

"Let your heart be joyous and pay homage to the Lord with thanksgiving for the beauty and wonder He has created for you. I tell you truly, one cannot walk in sunrise, or at sunset, or see the stars at night, without paying homage to a loving Father who has given life to all creation.

"When trouble comes and sorrow lays its hand upon you, look upon the beauty that surrounds you and lift your eyes toward heaven. Then shall the Heavenly Father comfort you and bring you peace.

Then Jesus rose and departed from them, for he wished that he might walk in that kingdom, which only he could see and hear.

FRIDAY NIGHT
THIRTEENTH INVOCATION – GOD
(Oneness with all Life)

During this final period of the sixth epoch, a new and spiritual mankind is beginning to rise from the ashes of human progression.

Dr. R. Maurice Bucke described this evolutionary process in his book *Cosmic Consciousness*:

> Cosmic Consciousness (unity with the consciousness of God) will become more and more universal and appear earlier in the individual life until the race at large will finally possess this faculty. The same race and not the same;

for a Cosmic Conscious race will not be the race which exists today, any more than the present race is the same which existed prior to the evolution of self consciousness.

"The simple truth is, that there has lived on the earth, appearing at intervals, for thousands of years among ordinary people, the first faint beginning of another race; walking the earth and breathing the air with us, but at the same time walking another earth and breathing another air of which we know little or nothing, but which is, all the same, our spiritual life, as its absence would be our spiritual death. This new race is in the act of being born from us, and in the near future it will occupy and possess the earth.

There is but one single way to ascend this ladder and enter into this final epoch of man's journey through matter. The way cannot be characterized by names such as philosophy, science, or even religion. However, each of these fields has provided a valuable stepping-stone toward this final phase of human evolution and progression. Even so, this path cannot be encompassed through any form of religious separation, for God is a God of the whole – not a God of only a part.

It is sufficient to note that Jesus left specific instructions on how to approach this gateway of tomorrow's world. He did not label it by country, religion, or belief, but with simple words to a simple people. Matthew 22:37-40:

> *"Jesus said unto him, Thou shalt love the Lord thy God with all thy heart, and with all thy soul, and with all thy mind*
>
> *"This is the first and great commandment.*
>
> *"And the second is like unto it, Thou shalt love thy neighbor as thyself.*
>
> *"On these two commandments hang all the law and the prophets."*

These rules are plainly spoken, but seem extremely difficult to live by. However, they were the underlying power that made Jesus what he was. He always speaks of a direct relationship with the Father. In his Invocation to God he more clearly defines a way to come into direct Invocation with the Lord of the Universe, not as a deity in the sky, but as a living breathing consciousness flowing through the entire universe.

On the evening of the Sabbath
Friday evening at sunset

Occasionally, the path became difficult for Jesus' disciples, because the purification of the body and soul caused that which was less in them to run undisciplined and unbridled like a wild animal.

When these hard times fell upon his followers, Jesus encouraged them, saying, "You must seek peace with the Kingdom of the Heavenly Father. Truly, you are born of your father by seed and of your mother by body. They reared you that you might find your true inheritance and know you are the descendant of a king.

"God is the Eternal Law, which fashioned the stars, the sun, the light and the darkness and He alone is the Lord of the soul. He is everywhere and there is nowhere that he is not.

"All which is in our understanding and all we know not, all is governed by the Law. The falling of the leaves, the flow of the rivers, and the music of the insects at night; these also are governed by the Law. There are many mansions in the Kingdom of heaven and many are the hidden things you cannot yet know.

"I tell you truly, the domain of God is so vast that no one can know its limits, for there are none. Yet the whole of His kingdom may be found in the smallest drop of dew on a flower, and in the scent of newly cut fields under the sun. There are no words to describe the Kingdom."

After spending a short time with his disciples at Capernaum, Jesus departed and went into Samaria to teach in the settlements near the rocky peaks of Mt. Ebal and Mt. Gerizim. There were three cities, Samaria, Shechem and Sychar, and all were beautifully situated in the wildness of the hill country.

Although Jesus visited all three cities, and even went as far as Bethany to the home of Lazarus and his sisters, he did not go to the Temple of Jerusalem, because there was a grave danger that he would be taken captive and it was not yet his time.

And it came to pass one evening when the sun was low in the sky the Master went with his disciples into the Garden of Gethsemane. When they had seated themselves in the olive grove one of his disciples asked, "Master how can we come closer to God and become as you?"

"Truly," Jesus replied, "the path to the heavenly kingdom is long and arduous, yet the doorway wherefore one might come unto the throne of God is easy, for it is open to all people. Love will unlock the door and your mind will carry you through its gate. When there is naught in you but the desire to see God, He will come to you and send His Holy Spirit that you might be prepared to enter His Kingdom."

"Why then, Master, is the path so difficult?" asked the disciple.

"You are encumbered by the ways of the world and your eyes are sealed, except for those things of the world," responded Jesus. "As we have sat thusly many times in the quietude of the evening, have we talked of naught else but of God and His Law?"

And his disciples nodded their heads, although their eyes were filled with questions.

Knowing that the disciples were as yet like children, Jesus looked upon them with great fortitude and began to speak once more, "Know you not that the earth and even the heavens above us are but God in visual form? See the space existing between the unnumbered stars? That is none other than the invisible realm of God and within that space there are many worlds you cannot yet see.

"God is a God of the living and can only be worshipped by the living, for He abides everywhere. When you breathe you breathe of His breath. When you plow your fields you move because of His power. Whenever you hear the birds sing you hear His voice. He is the ripple of the water touching the land, and He is the sweet scent of flowers filling the night air.

"But how can that be?" another disciple asked.

Jesus answered him softly, "You must practice the Invocations, for they are of God. And one day when the wind is hushed and the flower does not dance you will come face-to-face with God."

"Will I know?" asked the disciple.

"Yes," Jesus answered with great compassion," you will know. All the words over the seven kingdoms cannot describe Him, for He is both visible and invisible. Yet, every heart and every mind approaching Him through the open doorway of love will come unto His throne. Therefore, you must seek escape from the outer world by sealing off the sound and sights of that world.

"Now I say to you, close your eyes against the outer world that you might experience that inner world. In the eyes of your mind, think upon the Spirit that is now creating and sustaining all life, even the unnumbered stars.

"Feel yourself within yourself, for if you but knew it, this self is of God. Draw this power of God within you and allow it to envelop your soul and your mind. And you will not only feel, but you will also come to know the Holy Spirit of your Heavenly Father.

"And when He has entered to dwell with you offer your heart, your mind, and your soul, for these are the most worthy gifts of sacrifice. As you give, so shall He give back a thousand times even greater gifts.

"Do not give that you receive only, as that is the way of earth. Give of yourself because you wish to give and you shall feel a joy greater than any you have ever known.

"Know you that only those who seek God shall find Him, for

His Spirit does not come to dwell in those whose desires for worldly things are greater than their desires for the Kingdom of Heaven. Be not like the Scribes and Pharisees who seek worldly recognition for their piety.

"Allow your heart and your mind and your soul to flow toward the stars and become one with all creation. And then you shall become one with your Heavenly Father even as He shall become one with you, for all creation is one.

"Fear not when God sends forth His Holy Spirit to abide with you all the days of your life, for then you shall be purged and freed from all defilement. This is for your good that you might dwell with Him, and He with you forever and ever.

"One day you shall dwell in the Kingdom of Heaven, whether you are of earth, or whether you live in worlds unseen by earthly eyes.

"The Holy Spirit of the Heavenly Father has been with you always, but the door has been closed because each has been enticed by worldly things. You have now opened wide this door and it shall nevermore be closed."

And Jesus and his disciples sat together beneath the radiant stars and communed with the Spirit of the Heavenly Father. They knew not pain, or suffering, and possessed no awareness of existence. And for a time they were one with God and the universe was within them.

And when the disciples, who were with Jesus, returned to the world, the Sprit of God came also with them. And they entered unto the resurrection, for He who once was dead in them had now been raised.

Saturday Morning
Fourteenth Invocation – the Holy Earth
(Unity of Heaven and Earth)

The seventh day of creation will dawn and the Kingdom of the Heavenly Father will become one with the whole of earth through the resurrection of His Spirit within all people.

No one wrote about this extraordinary union more eloquently than John the Beloved in his Revelation 21:1-4:

"And I saw a new heaven and a new earth; for the first heaven and the first earth were passed away. And there was no more sea.

"And I John saw the holy city, New Jerusalem (the dawning of the seventh epoch in which human man is transformed into divine man) coming down from God out of heaven, prepared as a bride adorned for her husband (the purified souls, white and clean, prepared to become one with God).

"And I heard a great voice out of heaven, say, Behold the tabernacle of God is with men and he shall dwell with them and they shall be his people, and God himself shall be with them, and be their God.

"And God shall wipe away all tears from their eyes; and there shall be no more death, neither sorrow, nor crying, neither shall there be any more pain; for the former things are passed away (the world as it is today)."

Many people find it difficult to conceive that this world, which is engaged in so much conflict, shall one day become a world of peace and that all people will live together in harmony. Nonetheless, it will come to pass. Every great prophet has witnessed this coming of the next epoch. Someday perhaps even science will also conclude that this is the inevitable future of our world, if it has not already done so.

It is almost impossible to imagine what it will be like to live in a world where different religions, denominations, and sects no longer fight one another, and where the wars on earth have ceased because the soul has risen above hatred, anger, jealousy, and petty differences. Yet that was, and is, the very assignment instilled in earth's potential at the beginning of the universe.

Human cannot rise beyond human while there is hatred between people, wars between nations, or the soul is bound by worldly senses to those things, which bring upon it sorrow and pain. Yet, if one could travel back through time and view the earth as it was in the days of volcanic eruptions, molten gasses and venusian-like rain, it would be obvious that the world has also come a long way since the beginning.

Millions of years form mankind's past, but there are not millions of years in our future. The birth of reasoning has enabled the human race to open a doorway leading into the world of tomorrow. Stepping through that door should not be difficult. One has merely to awaken the Spirit of God within them, and this takes nothing more than a simple love of the soul for He who dwells in it. After all, the entire world has searched for God since reasoning proclaimed that the movement of the universe was subject to some invisible and intangible power.

There is little reference to the Invocation of the Holy Earth in the Lost Jesus Scroll, perhaps because the Sabbath, meaning cessation from exertion, is celebrated in various forms by a variety of religions. The practice of the Jewish Sabbath is an Invocation in itself. It is a means of binding these people who believe that they are the "chosen" people together, and thus keeping them apart from the rest of mankind.

First of all, according to Mosaic ritual, the Sabbath is to be observed by cessation of all labor, signifying that mankind has finished his work on earth and God now dwells with him. Trading is prohibited, and at one time the Law even required the Children of Israel to double their daily offering. Thus the Sabbath was, and still is; a day of gladness, a day of delight, and day spent paying homage to God through prayers and thanksgiving.

The day of the Sabbath
Saturday morning at sunrise

Although Jesus did not give specific instructions to his disciples pertaining to the Sabbath, he did say:

As you were once suckled and comforted by your mother when you were a child, but later went to join your father and his work when you had grown, so it is with earth. She is your Holy Mother and through her lessons you are guided toward Him who is your true father that you might know your true home and become true Sons of God.

Section Three

JESUS' TEACHINGS ON MERGER WITH THREE SACRED RIVERS (LIFE – SOUND – LIGHT)

SECTION THREE

Merger with the Sacred Rivers

Words cannot do justice to the few remaining pages of the *Lost Jesus Scroll*, for they present some of Jesus' most magnificent teachings. At the time these could best be taught to those who had a thorough understanding of the multitudinous forces that created and brought the universe into being. Therefore, Jesus relegated these to his "elect" who had received his deeper teachings.

✶✶✶

And it came to pass; as the wind blew once more from the south and the rains began to abate, the melting snows again made their way toward the Jordan River. The Feast of the Passover neared and Jesus knew that the last remaining pages of his life must soon close. He had gone to Capernaum to sit again by the rivers edge for the last time.

Early on the following morning after their arrival, as the bright sun began to cast its rays on the land, the disciples gathered again on the Shores of Galilee to await the coming of their Master. Looking up, they saw him approaching.

As Jesus neared he lifted his hand in greeting and then sat down among them, saying, "Soon I must depart from you. I have taught you those mysteries that will guide you to Him who has been with you since the beginning. Know you, if you will but follow in the path I have shown you, you will never be alone, or without comfort, or without the guidance of mighty angels.

"Yet, I would have you learn the deepest secrets of all. You have been as a child on a long journey and one day you looked up and realized that you had now reached manhood. Before I depart from you, I wish to instruct you on the three greatest Invocations of all.

"Three are the great rivers that will take you where few have ever gone. These are the Holy Rivers of Life, the Holy River of Sound and the Holy River of Light. I will teach you the ancient way to traverse them and you shall bathe in the light of heaven. Then all things will become known to you that were before only dreamed.

"In the hour before the rising sun, as the earth awakes, you must seek oneness with the Holy River of Life, that life, which exists through all creation.

"Remember your Brother Tree, for it is he who holds the key to the mystery of life. Embrace him as you have done in the past, and in the eye of your mind travel toward the new rising sun. Think upon that power that brought forth the sun and the earth, and observe the Holy River of Life as it gathers in the tree.

"As you embrace your Brother Tree, think only about the Holy River of Life that flows from the Heavenly Father throughout all creation. Draw this Holy River within you and you will merge with all life everywhere and be no more of the body.

As your thoughts flow outward, say the word 'Life." Forget all things, except that Spirit of the Heavenly Father flowing through you. This shall be for your healing and your health, but it shall also strengthen you for the long journey that yet lies ahead of you.

"I tell you truly, this power descends from God and exists throughout all life. It is the same power that makes miracles possible, for it alone enables the blind to see and the lame to walk. Yet, it is all around you.

"Even so, it takes the power of your body, your mind and your soul, to make manifest that which cannot be seen by human eyes."

Heeding the Master's instructions, the disciples sat silently and closed their eyes. They thought upon the force of life that ran throughout the earth, and how the roots of the plants drew this upward and received nourishment thereof. Finally it seemed as though earth became a living being. Her life force seemed to gather itself within the disciples and they felt a strength and power they had never known. In time they became one with life everywhere and the frailty of human existence passed from them.

✲✲✲

Later that day, when the sun was casting its radiance over the land and warming all things, Jesus, who had remained with his disciples since the early hour, began to teach once more.

"Hear you not the hush that has now come upon us?" Jesus asked. "That hush is sound itself, for it is only in the quiet of the day that we can hear the sound that brought forth creation.

"You must learn to hear beyond hearing, even as you must learn to see beyond seeing, in order to commune with the holy angels of God. Although the angels are ever with us, you see them not and you hear them not, even as you do not hear the sound that came in the beginning.

"When the Heavenly Father brought forth creation from Light, that Light also became sound. This sound consists of the earth and all that is upon earth, as well as the stars. It is like unto the humming of a bee, but it is not heard because the ears hear only the sounds of life, such as the wind soughing through the trees.

"But Master," a disciple asked, "The bee hums. Is this indeed the sound of the beginning and if so, then how can this be?"

And Jesus looked upon him with measure of amusement, as a father might look upon a child. "It is difficult for one who has never heard anything beyond those things of the world to understand that there was only one sound in the beginning, even as there was but one Law.

"From one Law came many laws and from one Sound came many sounds. Yet if all of the sounds from every star in the universe were heard at the same time, they would form but one sound. As laws have become many, so have the sounds become many. These are heard in all the music ever created or played, and in all the laws discussed by the Scribes and Pharisees.

"If we would hear the voices of angels and yea, even the voice of God, we must hear beyond the din and noise of the world.

"Think upon the distant streams as their water trickles over the rocks on their way to the sea. Hear the waves lap against the shore and listen to the sweet sound of this tree as it spreads out its roots below us."

"But Master," one of the disciples cried out, "How can I hear something that is so far away or something that has no sound. I cannot hear the sound of the tree beneath me, yet I hear its branches move in the wind."

"You cannot hear it, because your ears hear only the sound of my voice or the sound of my feet moving in the earth," Jesus replied. "See that tree in the distance, the one which branches almost touch the earth?"

"Yes," replied the disciple, "I see it."

"As you look upon the distant tree with your eyes, you must now reach out your ears to hear its sound," Jesus instructed.

"If you will but practice hearing beyond hearing, so will your ears develop the ability to hear the angels speak, for their voices are like the gentle rain touching the flowering plant, or the sweet fragrance of the flowers.

"It was meant that man and angel should walk together, for the angels are sent by the Heavenly Father to protect and guide all life to that realm where pain and sorrow are no more.

"Now close your eyes and listen with your ears for the flowing sound of the river as it meets the sea. Hear its happy song and hear it become quiet as it flows into the vaster sea, where it mingles in both body and sound.

"Allow your mind to travel to that point where the body and sound of the river joins the sea. Listen with new ears to the song that flows through the river and sea as they come together in joyous union.

"Travel in the eye of your mind and beyond hearing to the beginning of creation when the stars were first formed. Hear you not that one beautiful chord, which fills the empty space where life has not yet begun.

As your breath flows outward become one with the Great Ocean of Sound that was in the beginning. And you will feel the peace of God wash away all your pain and cares, for your body will no longer entrap you.

"One day you will both see and hear in that world which few have ever known."

As the disciples sat with Jesus along the river's edge, they closed their eyes. Soon they ceased to be aware of earth and the sounds of earth. Yet, they heard something new. Even the tree in a distance seemed to speak to them. It was as though it had become what it was before the earth came into being, a sound of splendor and wonder.

As Jesus watched those who were with him, he saw that they were no more of the body, for they had discovered the mystery of the holy river of sound.

✳✳✳

That night, as the disciples once again gathered with the Master, Jesus spoke to them saying. "Evening has come upon us and tomorrow we must leave that we might celebrate the Feast of the

Passover. Yet, there is one more river that you must learn to traverse and it is the greatest of all. It is the Holy River of Light. Once you have followed it to its source you will be born anew and walk where only angels walk.

"Thus, when darkness descends over the land and the stars come out in their splendor, and when the earth is bathed by the silence of the evening, it is then that you shall travel the greatest of the three rivers. It is a river from whence there is no return.

"I tell you truly, when you have merged with the Light of God, then shall that Light be with you evermore, and the world that you have known shall not be."

"Does this mean that we shall die?" someone asked.

"No, you shall not die as the body dies, but you shall die of those things that once brought you sorrow and pain. For this Light is the Light of God and was brought forth in the beginning. Without it there would be no life.

"Your bodies have been built by the Holy River of Life and it moves through you, even as it moves through the trees. Yet that part of you, which is not in the body, lives in a world you cannot see.

"Your eyes were not given you to see only those things you can touch and feel, but also to see and hear in a world you cannot see. I tell you truly, that world, which you cannot see, is your true home.

"When you body dies it returns to the dust of earth. But that life within you returns to your true home, for it cannot be killed, nor does it die.

"When night comes upon you, you fall asleep. Yet, even in your sleep, your soul returns to your true home, there to bathe in the eternal stream of light.

"Thus, before you close the eyes of your body, allow the eye of your mind to direct you toward the stars, for the stars reflect the Light of your Heavenly Father.

"With the eye of your mind, unfold your wings of light and

soar into the far-reaching wonder of untold suns. Know you not that your thoughts are as an arrow in the hands of the skilled archer who knows where his arrow goes.

"I tell you truly, where your mind travels, so do you. Learn therefore to become like he who knows where his arrow goes even before he sends it.

"Meld with the central core of the Holy Light, for there your Heavenly Father brings you unto himself. And in that moment you will no longer remember earth, but you will bathe in the Holy River of Light, which flows from God throughout all creation.

"Always before you sleep, seek to dwell in the arms of your Heavenly Father and you will be taught by His unknown angels. In the morning you shall rise and you shall know that which you knew not when sleep closed your eyes.

"Truly, the body is more than a body of dust and water; it is a chariot to drive forth into battle.

"Your ears are more than ears to hear only those things of earth. They were given to you to hear in both the world of angels and the world of man, and to enter into the holy sound that brought forth the world.

"And your eyes are not just eyes to see the grain on the distant hills, or the tree beneath you, but they were made to see the Holy Kingdom of the Heavenly Father.

"Only through the eyes of your mind can you travel to that place where earth is no more, and there dwell in your true home where death exists not and illness cannot come nigh you.

"One day your body will return to the dust from whence it was made. Then too shall your eyes and your ears disappear. When all these have gone, only then shall you find that you truly live, and only then shall you feel true joy and peace and a world without end.

"Know you not, you are more eternal than earth and all that is upon her, and you are more eternal than the heavens and all the stars therein. Death cannot kill your soul, nor can fire burn it, for your soul is born of the same Light that brought forth all creation.

"Truly, you are the temple of God and His Spirit dwells both within you and without you.

"And when all people have come unto the Light, then shall the world come into peace, as it was foretold by the great prophets of old."

After this Jesus lifted himself up from beneath the tree and when he had done so he looked down on his disciples with a deep abiding fondness, for he knew their time together was short. On the morrow they would leave for Jerusalem and the Feast of the Passover.

For a moment it seemed that the earth stood still and the river no more sang its joyful song, but wept as it moved toward the darkening sea.

Jesus raised his hand in farewell, saying, "Peace be with you."

BIBLIOGRAPHY

Apocrypha. Cambridge at University Press, Great Britain.

The Apocryphal New Testament. Translated by Dr. Montague Rhode James, Litt. D., F.B.A., F.S.A. Provost of Eton, Oxford University Press, London, England, 1926.

Apocryphal New Testament. William Wake, M.R., D.D., Archbishop of Canterbury, and Rev. Nathaniel Lardner, D.D., published by Simkin Marshall, Hamilton, Kent and Co., Glasgow, Scotland.

Apocryphal New Testament. Simpkin, Marshall, Hamilton, Kent and Co., London, England.

The Archko Volume or *The Archeological Writings of the Sanhedrin and Talmud of the Jews.* Translated by Drs. McIntosh and Twyman, Keats Publishing, Inc., New Canaan, Connecticut. 1975.

Augustine. Robert Meagher, New York University, 1978

Augustine of Hippo. Peter Brown, University of California Press, 1978

Babylonian Genesis. Alexander Heidel, University of Chicago Press, Chicago and London, 1942.

Bible as History. Werner Keller, 1909, Translated from German by William Neil. Published by William Morrow and Co., Inc., N.Y.

Book of Enoch. R.H. Charles, D. Litt., D.D., Clarendon Press, 1964

Complete Works – The Second Birth. Omraam Mikhael Aivanhov Prosveta, U.S.A. edition.

Day Christ Died. Jim Bishop, Harper and Row, San Francisco.

Dead Sea Scrolls. Edmund Wilson, Oxford University Press, 1969.

Dead Sea Scrolls and the Bible. Charles F. Pfeiffer, Baker Book House Co., 1969.

Dead Sea Scrolls and the Christian Myth. John M. Allegro, Westbridge Books, 1979.

DeSanto Joseph at Arimathea. Emperor Heodusia (found in Pilate's Praelorium in Jerusalem - AD 379)

Drama of the Last Disciples. George F. Jowett, Published by Covenant Publishing Co., Ltd., London, England, 1975.

Eusebius, History of the Church from Christ to Constantine. Translated by G.A. Williamson, Penguin, 1965.

Gods, Graves and Scholars, History of Archaeology. C.C. Ceram. Bantam Books, 1967.

Galilean –A Life of Christ. Albert DePina, House-Warven Publishers, Hollywood,

Gospel According to Thomas. Coptic Text, translated by A. Guillaumont and Yassah Abd Al Masih, Harper and Row, New York, 1959.

Harper Bible Dictionary. Madeline S. Miller and J. Lane Miller, Harper and Row, New York, 1973.

Hebraic Tongue Restored. Fabre d'Olivet, Samuel Weiser, Inc., York Beach, Maine, 1976

History of the Britons. Nennius, England, 796.

History of the First Council of Nice. Dean Dudley, Attorney at Law, Copyright A.D. 1886, published by Peter Echler Publishing Co., 1925.

Holy Bible from Ancient Eastern Manuscripts. Translated from the Peshitta by George M. Lamsa, 1933, Published by A.J. Holman Company, Nashville, Tennessee.

Holy Bible. Translated out of original tongues by His Majesty's King James special command. Printed by His Majesty's Printer, Eyre and Spottiswoode, Ltd., London, England.

Holy Kabbalah. A.E. Waite, University Books, Citadel Press.

Introduction to the Cabala – Tree of Life. Z'ev ben Shimon Halevi, Samuel Weiser, Inc., New York, 1972.

Israel and the Dead Sea Scrolls. Edmond Wilson, Farrar, Straus and Giroux, New York, 1978.

Israelites. Time Life Books, catalogue card no. 75-4101.

Jerusalem History Atlas. Martin Gilbert, MacMillan Publishing Co., New York.

Jesus. Michael Grant, Weidenfeld and Nicholson, London.

Joseph of Arimathea. Skeats, University Press, 1871.

Josephus Complete Works: Antiquities of the Jews and the War of the Jews. Translated by William Whiston, A.M. 1867. Published by Porter and Coates, Philadelphia, Pennsylvania..

Letters of the Younger Pleny. Translated by Betty Radiel, Penguin Books, 1963.

Life of St. Mary Magdelene. Maurus Rabanus, Archbishop of Meyenie, England.

Lives of the Saints. Translated by J.F. Webb, Penguin Books, 1965.

The Lost Years of Jesus Revealed. Rev. Dr. Charles Francis Potter, Fawcett Publications, Inc., 1962.

Magna Tabula Glastoniae. Pynson(currently in possession of the House of Howard) England.

Metrical Life of St. Joseph. Pynson, England, 1520.

Morals and Dogma of the Ancient and Accepted Scottish Rite of Freemasonry. Prepared for the council of the Thirty-third Degree. Entered into the Library of Congress at Washington, D.C., 1871, published by L.H. Jenkins, Inc., Richmond, Virginia.

Mystical Doctrine of St. John of the Cross. Selected by R.H.J. Stewart, Sheed and Ward, London.

Nag Hammadi Library. Translated by members of the Coptic Gnostic Library Project of the Institute for Antiquity and Christianity, Harper and Row Publishers, New York, 1977.

New Testament Apocrypha. Edited by Professor Wilhelm Schneemelcher, University of Bonn. English translation edited by R. Wilson, Ph.D. Theology, Westminster Press, Philadelphia, Pennsylvania.

Odes of Solomon: Original Christianity Revealed. Robert Winterhalter, Llewellyn Publications, St. Paul, Minnesota, 1985.

Old Testament Light. George M. Lamsa, Harper and Row, 1893.

Orthodox Church. Timothy Ware, Penguin Books, 1963.

Oxford Dictionary of Saints. David Hugh Farmer, Oxford University Press, 1978.

Pagan and Christian Creeds: Their Origin and Meaning. Edward Carpenter, Harcourt Brace and Co., New York.

Philo of Alexandria. Samuel Sandmel, Oxford University Press, New York, 1979

Primitive Christianity, Vols. I, II, III, and IV. Otto Pfleiderer, D.D., Reference Book Publishers, Inc., New Jersey, 1965.

Shroud. Robert K. Wilson, Bantam Books, 1977.

The Shroud of Turin. Ian Wilson, Doubleday and Co., Inc., New York, 1979.

Southern Palestine and Jerusalem. W.M. Thomson, Harper and Brothers, 1982.

St. Francis of Assisi. Morris Bishop, Little Brown and Co., Boston, 1974.

St. Joseph of Arimathea at Glastonbury. Kiovel Smithett Lewis, late Vicar of Glastonbury, published by James Clarke and Co., Cambridge, England, 1922.

Unger's Bible Dictionary. Merrill F. Unger, 1957-1980, Moody Press, Chicago, Illinois.

Westminster Dictionary of the Bible. John D. Davis, Ph.D., D.D., Westminster Press, Philadelphia, 1944.

Wild Branch on the Olive Tree. Father William Treacy and Rabbi Raphael Levine in collaboration with Sister Patricia Jacobsen, Binford and Mort Publishers.

Wycliffe Bible Commentary. Edited by Charles F. Pfeifer – Old Testament, and Everett F. Harrison, New Testament, Moody Press, Chicago, Illinois, 1962

INDEX

A'bib (Abib), 53
Africanus Australopithecus, 126
Alexandria, 15, 168
Altar of fire, 42
Andrew, 54
Angels of the Heavenly Father, 23,
Anna, 55
Antiochus Epiphanes, 19
Antiquities of the Jews, 28, 167
Apocryphal New Testament, 20, 165
Apocryphal New Testament, 20
Apostolic Constitution, 14
Archelaus, 15
Ark of the Covenant, 42
Austrian Government, 22

Banus, 12
Battle of Armageddon, 37
Bethany, 55, 106, 149
Bethlehem, 55
Big Bang, 112
Book of James, 34
Bordeaux, Edmond S., 14, 20, 21, 23, 25
Brother Tree, 139, 158
Brotherhood, 22, 23, 30-32, 45, 97, 98, 135
Bucke, R. Maurice, Dr., 146

Caesarea, 15
Capernaum, 54, 81, 87, 91, 133, 135, 148, 157
Catechumens, 15
Chorazin, 81
Clemens, 14
Confession of Pontius Pilate, 20
Corinthians, 127
Cosmic Consciousness, 118, 122, 146
creative power, 112
Creative Principle, 30, 36, 122
Creative Work, 10, 46, 132, 133, 135-137
Cyril, 15

Dead Sea, 28, 29, 33, 35, 45, 133-134, 165, 166
Dead Sea Scriptures, 45
Dead Sea Scrolls, 28, 29, 33, 35, 165, 166
Divine Plan, 39-41, 76, 110, 112, 114, 132, 143

Edom, 134
Egypt, 31, 55
Elders, 30, 34
eleventh hour, 133
Ell es-sultan, 134
Eluh, 88
end time, 38, 41
Epochs, 41
Essen, 27
Essene Community, 30, 31, 34
Essene Jesus, 19, 20
Essene Sect, 19, 28, 31, 33
Eternal Law, 148
Ethanim, 54

Feast of the Passover, 105, 157, 164
Feast of Unleavened Bread, 105
Flavius Josephus, 18, 28, 29
Franciscan Monks, 22

Galaxies, 124, 127, 130
Galilee, 7, 37, 38, 53, 54, 81, 98, 107, 113, 158
Garden of Eden, 84
Garden of Gethsemane, 54, 128, 149
Garden of the Brotherhood, 97, 135
Genesis II, 127
gift of tongues, 108
Great Plan, 124, 130
Great Sea, 111, 118
great sea, 95, 123, 130
Great Work, 43, 115

Habsburgs, 22
Hammath, 81

Hebrew High Priest, 27
Hebron, 55
Hippo, 15, 165
Holy Beings, 29
Holy of the Holies, 40, 42
Holy River of Life, 158, 162
Holy River of Light, 158, 162, 163
Holy River of Sound, 158, 161
Holy Temple, 34, 89, 108
Homo sapien, 126
House of Misery
Hymn of the Initiates

Ijar, 88
Illumination, 39
Immortals, 121
indwelling divine nature, 141
Invocations, Introduction, 103
    Saturday night, Power, 109
    Sunday morning, Sun, 112
    Sunday night, Love, 114
    Monday morning, Water, 118
    Monday night, Wisdom, 120
    Tuesday morning, Air, 124
    Tuesday night, Eternal Life, 126
    Wednesday, morning, Earth, 129
    Wednesday night, Creative Work, 132
    Thursday, morning, Life, 137
    Thursday night, Peace, 140
    Friday, morning, 143
    Friday, night, 146

Israel, 27, 30, 31, 34, 39, 53, 54, 91, 137, 153, 166

Jericho, 53, 107, 134, 135
Jerusalem, 15, 34, 54, 55, 81, 104, 107, 149, 164-166,
Jesus, brother of Onias, 19
Jesus, son of Damneus, 19
Jesus, son of Gamala, 19
Jesus, son of Gamaliel, 19
Jesus, son of Thebuthus, 19
Jesus the Christ, 19, 20, 33
Jesus, the eldest priest after Ananus, 19

Jesus, the son of Phabet, 18
Jesus, the son of Saphat, 19
Jesus, the son of Sapphias, 18
Joachim, 55
John the Baptist, 55
John the Beloved, 33, 38, 39, 42, 47, 152
Jordon, 53-55, 57, 67, 81, 107, 133-134, 157
Joseph, Father to Jesus, 34
Joseph of Arimathea, 166
Joseph ben Matthias, 28
Judaic, 27
Judgment, 37, 93, 115

Kelt, 133, 134
khamassen, 81
King David, 81

laver of water, 42
Law of God, 42, 83, 84, 141
Laws of Moses, 28, 84, 106
Lazarus, 55, 106, 133, 149
Lebanon, 53, 107
Letter, The, Pope John Paul II, 24
Letter, The, eyewitness account, 20
light (intellectual elementizing), 41
Light of Consciousness, 41
Lost Jesus Scroll,
    Discovery, 23
    Essene correlation, 35
    Invocation of the Angels, 35
    John the Beloved, 47
    The mysteries revealed, 38

Magadan, 81
Magdala, 81
Manichaeans, 15
Manual of Discipline, 29, 35
Marcheshvan, 88
Mary, 55
Matthew, 120, 147
Mercati, Monsignor, 22
Mesopotamia, 15
Messiah, 34

Metamorphosis, 38, 40, 42, 43
Milan, 15
Moab, 134
Mondik, Monsignor, 22
Monsignor G.B. Re, Assessor, 24
Mosaic Law, 105
Moses, 16, 23, 27-29, 34, 38-40, 42, 45, 46, 71, 72, 83, 84, 91, 106, 111, 127, 137, 145
Mount of Olives, 54
Mt. Ebal, 149
Mt. Gerizim, 149
Mt. Olivet, 55

Nahum, 55
Natural & Cosmic Law, 105,
Nature of the Universe, 14, 17, 112
New Essenes, 19
New Jerusalem, 104, 152
Nisan, 53, 105
Old Testament, 33, 167, 168
Order, Essene, 27, 29

Pairist Order, 22
Patience, 30, 118
Pathways to Inner Peace, 91
Peace with Culture, 46, 97
Peace with the Body, 46, 95
Peace with the Family, 46, 96
Peace with the Heavenly Father, 46, 98
Peace with the Holy Earth, 98
Peace with Mind, 46
Peace with the World, 97
Perseverance, 118, 119
Peter, 54, 90, 111, 165
Pharisees, 28, 32, 61, 71, 73, 84, 97, 108, 122, 151, 160
philosopher's stone, 121
Pope John Paul II, 22, 24
Prefect of the Archives of the Roman Vatican, 22
Prior, 22
Prophets, 147, 164
Prototype, 112
Psalms of David, 23

Quarnantana, 134
Qumran, 28, 29, 30, 33

raised the dead, 47, 141
Rakkath, 81
Regula Santa, 22
Resurrection of the Dead, 37, 38
Rev: 21:1-4, 152
Revelation, 16, 18, 38, 39, 42, 104, 152
Room of the Holies, 40, 42
Royal Archives of the Habsburgs, 22

Sabbath, 46, 104, 132, 133, 136, 153
Sadducees, 32, 71
Samaria, 148, 149
Sanhedrin Council, 31
Scribes, 61, 71, 73, 84, 108, 109, 122, 151, 160
Scriptorium, 23
Secretary of the Roman Vatican, 23
seven prong candlestick, 40, 42
seventh day, 41, 104, 127, 132, 133, 151
seventh epoch, 38, 41, 46, 127, 132, 133, 143, 144, 152
Shechem, 149
Simon, 54, 90, 111
Simon Peter, 90
Sinai Peninsula, 39
Sivan, 57, 88
Slavonic, 22
Solar systems, 112, 124
Sons of Heaven, 29
Spinelli, Mario, 24
Spirit of God, 40, 42, 110, 111, 127, 153
spiritual education, 140
Spring Equinox, 53, 105
St. Augustine, 15, 165
St. Ambrose, 15
St. Basil, 15
St. Benedict, 22, 23
St. Cyril, 15
St. Dionysius, 14
St. Francis of Assisi, 22, 168
St. Jerome, 22, 23
St. John, of the Cross, 167
St. John's Revelation, 18, 38, 39, 42, 104

Tabernacle in the Wilderness, 39, 40, 42, 45
Tammuz, 54, 81, 91
Teacher of Righteousness, Moses, 28
Temple of Jerusalem, 34, 55, 149
Tertullian, 15
The War of the Jews, 28, 167
Thomas, 116, 117, 166
Thoughts, 68, 89, 95, 96, 106, 112, 142, 158, 163
Tiberius, 86
Transformation, 16, 18, 21, 24, 37-39, 45, 144
Tree of Life, 40, 42, 45, 166
twelve o'clock, 133
twelve tribes of Israel, 39

Venus, 129, 153
Violence, 82, 83

Zacharias, 55
"Zadokite" Document, 28

www.ingramcontent.com/pod-product-compliance
Lightning Source LLC
Chambersburg PA
CBHW031643040426
42453CB00006B/191